Tim Demuth

The Spread of
London's Underground

Capital Transport

Introduction

A cut and cover section of the Metropolitan Railway under construction at King's Cross and on the site of the original platforms, just east of the main line station which can be seen in the background. This is now the site of King's Cross Thameslink station.

By the middle of the nineteenth century most of the main line railways had established their terminal stations in the positions they still occupy today. Lines entering London from the north had been banned by the government from building their terminal stations to the south of the Euston Road. The Great Western, which had originally planned to share Euston station with the London & Birmingham Railway, instead opened their own station in 1854 at Paddington which was then a suburb in the west of London. Railways entering London from the south were barred from extending much further than the north bank of the Thames by the high cost of compensating landowners in the City of London. Lines from the east were able to reach the City's eastern boundary by demolishing and driving through poor housing districts. The wealth of the City was the magnet that the railway companies vied with each other to reach as carriers of goods as well as passengers. Because of the distance between the City and the terminal stations of the railways from the north and the west, road traffic connecting them to it and the emerging fashionable West End were clogging the thoroughfares.

The idea of a railway running entirely in tunnels beneath the streets came from a City solicitor, Charles Pearson, who set about persuading the public that his scheme was practicable. He managed to raise capital from the City of London as well as from the Great Western Railway, which was keen to have a rail connection with the City from its outlying terminus at Paddington, for the onward carriage from the west of passengers and freight, mainly meat and vegetables to feed the growing metropolis. The North Metropolitan Railway Company was therefore incorporated in 1853 to build a line of 3 ½ miles (5.6km) between Paddington and Farringdon Street with intermediate stations at Edgware Road (where the engine sheds and works were to be situated), Baker Street, Portland Road, Gower Street and

King's Cross – all of which were to be completed by 1858. Shortly after receiving Parliamentary powers to build the line the company was re-incorporated as the Metropolitan Railway Company. Cut and cover construction was possible for most of the way between Paddington and King's Cross, since the route ran mainly beneath roads. At Farringdon Street space for a terminal became available by the removal of the City Cattle Market to Islington, which also allowed the City Corporation to erect a central meat market at Smithfield. The Great Western was quick to acquire the lease on its basement for its City goods depot which would be served by means of the new subterranean railway.

Initially, Great Western broad gauge trains provided the Metropolitan's service. The line was originally laid with broad gauge tracks of 7ft 0¼in (2139mm) interlaced with standard gauge tracks of 4ft 8½in (1435mm), which enabled connecting standard gauge railways to reach their own City depots. This was to prove fortunate, since only six months after the opening of the line, on 10 January 1863, the Great Western gave just one week's notice of its intention to withdraw its provision of trains. The standard gauge Great Northern, through their junction to the west of King's Cross, filled the breach by loaning some of their

engines and coaches to run the line until the Metropolitan Railway's own standard gauge trains were ready to take over the operation in 1867.

On 1 October 1863 GNR and GWR trains started running from their respective out of town stations, by way of the Metropolitan Railway's tracks, to terminate in the City. In 1867 the Metropolitan had more engines and carriages built to run a joint service with the GWR to Hammersmith and, by 1884, around the Circle Line.

This book shows, in diagrammatic map form, how London's Underground system developed from its beginning in 1863 until the close of the twentieth century. Each spread covers a ten year period. The maps on the right of each spread show the situation at the close of that decade. However, any developments during a particular decade that did not survive to its end and some that were planned but did not materialise until the following decade are also shown. Lines are colour coded in today's familiar hues, while station names and railway company nomenclature reflect that in use at the close of the span of each map. Punctuation within station names follows today's practice since its use on maps and signing has varied considerably over the years.

The text on each spread includes lists of stations opened, closed and any that changed their names within the decade. Within those lists, names in italics give the dates that stations were originally opened by the railways that owned them, before becoming part of the Underground network.

Thanks are due to Mike Horne who made available his invaluable database of station opening, re-naming and closure dates, and to Peter Nichols who kindly spared his time and knowledge to check the information contained in this book. A single map giving dates of all changes to the Underground network is Doug Rose's London Underground Diagrammatic History, recommended as complementary to the information within this book. Help with up to date information on future planned railway routes was researched and provided to me by my former work colleague, Kim Kavanah, to whom I am also grateful. Finally, thanks to Capital Transport for suggesting this book as well as providing information and encouragement.

Tim Demuth, January 2003

All photographs are copyright
London's Transport Museum, except:
pages 8, 10, 16 – commercial postcards
page 18 centre left and top right.
28, 30 – Capital Transport
page 20 left – B T Cooke
page 20 right – J H Meredith
page 22 bottom left – Colour Rail

ISBN 185414 266 6
Published by
Capital Transport Publishing,
38 Long Elmes, Harrow Weald, Middlesex
Layout and maps designed by
Tim Demuth
Printed by CS Graphics, Singapore
© Capital Transport Publishing
  and Tim Demuth 2003

Abbreviations of railway companies used in the text and on maps

A&BR	Aylesbury & Buckingham Railway 1868–1891
BS&WR	Baker Street & Waterloo Railway (Bakerloo) 1906–1910
BR	British Railways / British Rail 1948–1996
CLR	Central London Railway 1900–1933
CCE&HR	Charing Cross Euston & Hampstead Railway 1907–1910
C&SLR	City & South London Railway 1890–1933
DLR	Docklands Light Railway 1987–
ECR	Eastern Counties Railway 1839–1862
ELR	East London Railway 1884–1947
GCR	Great Central Railway 1897–1922
GER	Great Eastern Railway 1862–1922
GNP&BR	Great Northern Piccadilly & Brompton Railway 1906–1910
GNR	Great Northern Railway 1848–1922
GW&GCJt	Great Western & Great Central Joint Railway 1899–1947
GWR	Great Western Railway 1838–1947
H&CR	Hammersmith & City Railway 1864–1867
LBSC	London Brighton & South Coast Railway 1840–1922
LCDR	London Chatham & Dover Railway 1859–1899
LER	London Electric Railway 1910–1933
LMS	London Midland & Scottish Railway 1923–1947
LNER	London & North Eastern Railway 1923–1947
LNWR	London & North Western Railway 1846–1922
LSWR	London & South Western Railway 1839–1922
LPTB	London Passenger Transport Board 1933–1947
LT	London Transport 1933–1996
LTSR	London Tilbury & Southend Railway 1854–1920
MetR	Metropolitan Railway 1863–1933
MDR	Metropolitan District Railway 1868–1933
Met&GCJt	Metropolitan & Great Central Joint Committee 1906–1947
MR	Midland Railway 1844–1922
NLR	North London Railway 1853–1922
O&AT	Oxford & Aylesbury Tramroad 1888–1899
SECR	South Eastern & Chatham Railway 1899–1922
SER	South Eastern Railway 1843–1899
SR	Southern Railway 1923–1948
W&CR	Waterloo & City Railway 1893–1907
WLR	West London Railway 1844–1947
WLER	West London Extension Railway 1863–1947
WT	Wotton Tramway 1871–1888

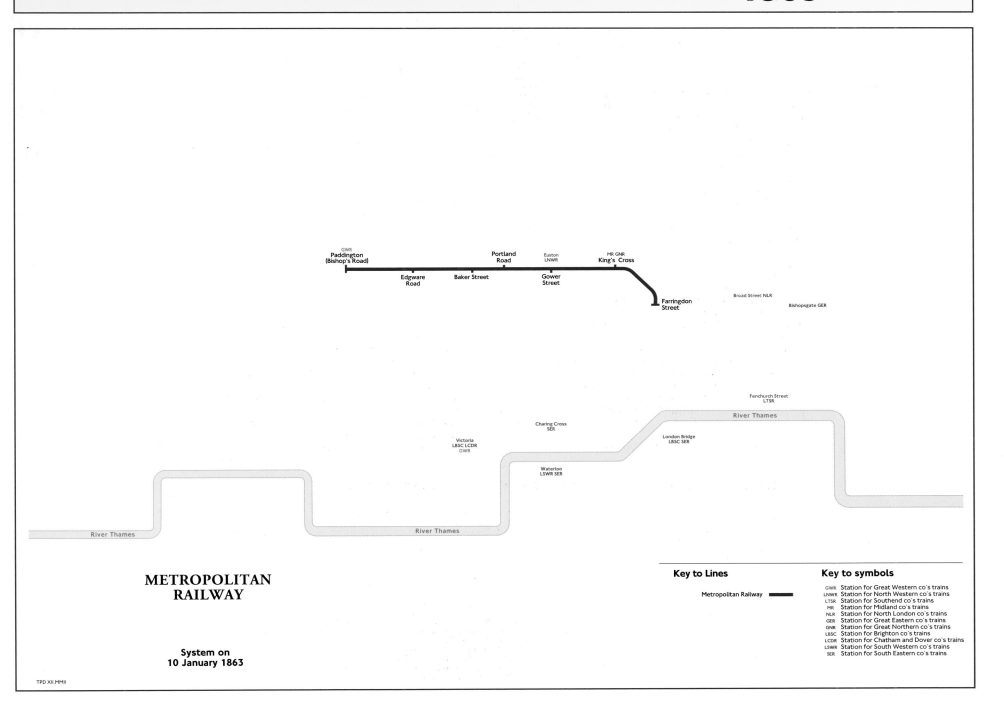

GWR
Paddington
(Bishop's Road)

Portland
Road

Euston
LNWR

MR GNR
King's Cross

Edgware
Road

Baker Street

Gower
Street

Farringdon
Street

Broad Street NLR

Bishopsgate GER

Fenchurch Street
LTSR

River Thames

Charing Cross
SER

London Bridge
LBSC SER

Victoria
LBSC LCDR
GWR

Waterloo
LSWR SER

River Thames

River Thames

**METROPOLITAN
RAILWAY**

**System on
10 January 1863**

TPD XII.MMII

Key to Lines

Metropolitan Railway ▬▬▬

Key to symbols

GWR Station for Great Western co's trains
LNWR Station for North Western co's trains
LTSR Station for Southend co's trains
MR Station for Midland co's trains
NLR Station for North London co's trains
GER Station for Great Eastern co's trains
GNR Station for Great Northern co's trains
LBSC Station for Brighton co's trains
LCDR Station for Chatham and Dover co's trains
LSWR Station for South Western co's trains
SER Station for South Eastern co's trains

Principal developments

Below A train of Metropolitan rolling stock using the standard gauge rails on the dual gauge H&CR at Hammersmith station.

Bottom These massive flyunders and bridges still survive to the west of Farringdon station. A GNR engine on the widened lines passes under a Metropolitan train heading for King's Cross, under the arch of Ray Street.

Bottom right The Metropolitan Railway's Notting Hill Gate station at the time of its opening in 1868. To this day it retains its arched overall glazed roof, although the end panels are now removed.

1863 First section of the Metropolitan Railway opened between Paddington Bishop's Road and Farringdon with intermediate stations at Edgware Road, Baker Street, Portland Road (now Great Portland Street), Gower Street (Euston Square) and King's Cross on 10 January. It was worked by the Great Western Railway using their broad track gauge trains, until 10 August. From that date the GWR trains were replaced by standard track gauge trains hired from the Great Northern Railway until the Metropolitan Railway's own trains became available.

1863 Through GWR broad gauge service commenced between Farringdon Street, Paddington Bishop's Road and Windsor from 1 October.

1863 Junction constructed at King's Cross connecting Great Northern Railway with the Metropolitan Railway, enabling Great Northern trains to run into Farringdon Street, opened on 1 October.

1864 Hammersmith & City Railway is opened between Green Lane Junction (Westbourne Park) and Hammersmith on 13 June, initially being worked by the Great Western Railway.

1865 Metropolitan Railway extended from Farringdon Street to Moorgate on 23 December.

1867 Formerly independent Hammersmith & City Railway

vested jointly with the Metropolitan and Great Western railways, being worked by the Metropolitan Railway from 1 July.

1868 St John's Wood Railway opened between Baker Street and Swiss Cottage on 13 April.

1868 The Metropolitan Railway built a junction between Edgware Road and Paddington (Bishop's Road) allowing them to continue a line southwards through the fashionable district of Kensington, with stations at Paddington (Praed Street), Bayswater, Notting Hill Gate, Kensington (High Street) and Brompton (Gloucester Road). It opened on 1 October. The section from Gloucester Road to an end-on connection with the District Railway at South Kensington was opened on 24 December.

1868 The Metropolitan District Railway opened its first section between Westminster Bridge and South Kensington, with intermediate stations at St James's Park, Victoria (for the adjoining London Brighton & South Coast and London Chatham & Dover railways' terminal stations) and Sloane Square on 24 December, making an end-on junction with the Metropolitan Railway's Kensington High Street branch.

1869 The GWR broad gauge service between the City and Windsor via Paddington suspended on 15 March. The service was resumed with standard gauge trains on 1 June.

1870 Metropolitan District Railway opens its line under the Victoria Embankment (which was constructed at the same time as part of the project) from Westminster to Blackfriars, with stations at Charing Cross and The Temple on 30 May.

Opening dates of stations, name changes and closures

Stations opened or first served

10.01.1863	Baker Street [H&C]	MetR
10.01.1863	Edgware Road	MetR
10.01.1863	Farringdon Street	MetR *first site*
10.01.1863	Gower Street	MetR
10.01.1863	King's Cross	MetR *first site*
10.01.1863	Paddington (Bishop's Road)	MetR
10.01.1863	Portland Road	MetR
13.06.1864	Hammersmith	H&CR *first site*
13.06.1864	Notting Hill	H&CR
13.06.1864	Shepherd's Bush	H&CR
1.07.1864	Kensington [WLR]	H&CR *first served*
24.04.1865	*Loughton [GER] present site*
23.12.1865	Aldersgate Street	MetR
23.12.1865	Farringdon Street	MetR *present site*
23.12.1865	Moorgate Street	MetR
1.02.1866	Westbourne Park	H&CR *first site*
22.08.1867	*East Finchley [GNR]*
1.04.1867	*Finchley Central [GNR] as Finchley & Hendon*
1.04.1867	*Mill Hill East [GNR] as Mill Hill*
13.04.1868	Marlborough Road	MetR
13.04.1868	St.John's Wood Road	MetR
13.04.1868	Swiss Cottage	MetR
23.09.1868	*Grandborough Road [A&BR]*
23.09.1868	*Quainton Road [A&BR] first site*
23.09.1868	*Verney Junction [A&BR]*
23.09.1868	*Winslow Road [A&BR]*
1.10.1868	Bayswater	MetR
1.10.1868	Brompton (Gloucester Road)	MetR
1.10.1868	Kensington (High Street)	MetR
1.10.1868	Notting Hill Gate	MetR
1.10.1868	Paddington (Praed Street)	MetR
1.12.1868	Hammersmith	MetR
1.10.1869	*Gunnersbury [LSWR]*
1.10.1869	*Kew Gardens [LSWR]*
1.10.1869	*Hammersmith (Grove Road) [LSWR]*
1.10.1869	*Shaftesbury Road [LSWR]*
1.10.1869	*Turnham Green [LSWR]*
24.12.1868	St.James's Park	MDR
24.12.1868	Sloane Square	MDR
24.12.1868	South Kensington	MetR
24.12.1868	Victoria	MDR
24.12.1868	Westminster Bridge	MDR
12.04.1869	Brompton (Gloucester Road)	MDR
12.04.1869	West Brompton	MDR
1.11.1869	Uxbridge Road	H&CR
30.05.1870	Blackfriars	MDR
30.05.1870	Charing Cross	MDR
30.05.1870	The Temple	MDR

Station names changed

from		*to*
1868	Kensington [WLR]	Kensington (Addison Road)
1869	Notting Hill	Notting Hill (Ladbroke Grove)
12.04.1864	Brompton (Gloucester Road)	Gloucester Road (Brompton)

Stations closed

22.12.1865	Farringdon Street	MetR *first site*
1.12.1868	Hammersmith	MetR *first site*

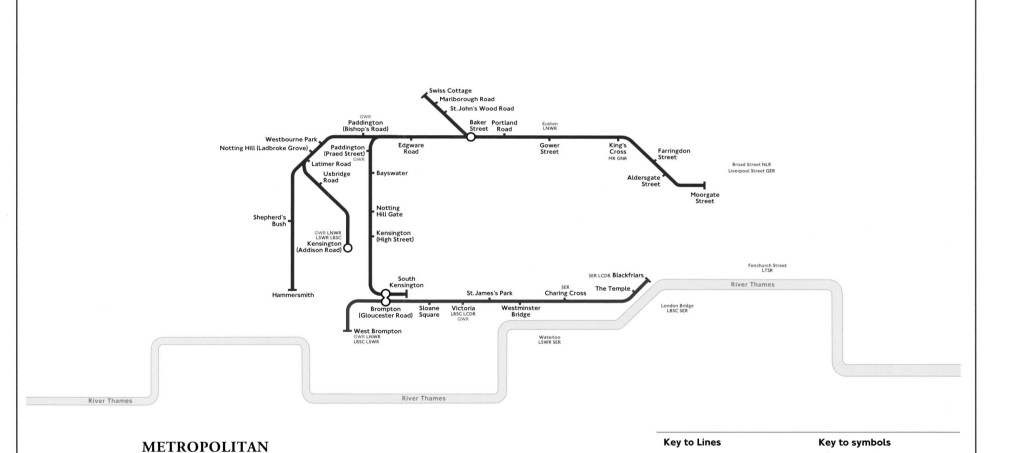

Swiss Cottage
Marlborough Road
St. John's Wood Road

GWR
Paddington
(Bishop's Road)

Baker Portland
Street Road

Euston
LNWR

Westbourne Park
Notting Hill (Ladbroke Grove)

Paddington
(Praed Street)
GWR

Edgware
Road

Gower
Street

King's
Cross
MR GNR

Farringdon
Street

Broad Street NLR
Liverpool Street GER

Latimer Road

Uxbridge
Road

Bayswater

Aldersgate
Street

Moorgate
Street

Shepherd's
Bush

Notting
Hill Gate

GWR LNWR
LSWR LBSC
Kensington
(Addison Road)

Kensington
(High Street)

Fenchurch Street
LTSR

SER LCDR Blackfriars

River Thames

Hammersmith

South
Kensington

SER
Charing Cross

The Temple

St. James's Park

London Bridge
LBSC SER

Brompton
(Gloucester Road)

Sloane
Square

Victoria
LBSC LCDR
GWR

Westminster
Bridge

Waterloo
LSWR SER

West Brompton
GWR LNWR
LBSC LSWR

River Thames

River Thames

METROPOLITAN
AND
METROPOLITAN DISTRICT
RAILWAYS

**System on
31 December 1870**

Key to Lines

District Railway ▬▬

Metropolitan Railway ▬▬

Key to symbols

○   Exchange stations
GWR   Station for Great Western co's trains
LNWR   Station for North Western co's trains
LTSR   Station for Southend co's trains
MR   Station for Midland co's trains
NLR   Station for North London co's trains
GER   Station for Great Eastern co's trains
GNR   Station for Great Northern co's trains
LBSC   Station for Brighton co's trains
LCDR   Station for Chatham and Dover co's trains
LSWR   Station for South Western co's trains
SER   Station for South Eastern co's trains

TPD XII.MMII

Principal developments of the decade

1871 The first part of the Duke of Buckingham's private project opened between Quainton Road and Wotton on 1 April 1871. The line was extended to its terminus at Brill in the summer of 1872. The Wotton Tramway was later worked (but not owned) by the Metropolitan Railway.

1871 Section of MDR opened between Blackfriars and Mansion House (which had its name altered from Cannon Street before the opening) on 3 July.

1871 District Railway opened branch from High Street Kensington to Earl's Court on 3 July.

1872 LNWR Outer Circle service, Broad Street to Mansion House via Willesden Junction, Addison Road and the link built by the MDR in 1869 to Earl's Court, commenced on 1 August.

1872 GWR Middle Circle service, Moorgate Street to Mansion House via Paddington, Edgware Road, Addison Road and Earl's Court, commenced on 1 August (withdrawn 1905).

1874 District Railway opened section from Earl's Court to Hammersmith on 9 August 1874.

1875 Metropolitan Railway extended their line from Moorgate Street to Liverpool Street (Great Eastern Railway station), where a junction was made with the Great Eastern Railway, on 1 February.

1875 The Metropolitan Railway also extended from Moorgate Street to Bishopsgate (the present Liverpool Street Circle Line station) on 12 July.

1876 Metropolitan Railway extended from Bishopsgate to Aldgate on 18 November.

1877 Extension opened to Ravenscourt Road to connect MDR to LSWR route to Richmond, over which District Line trains have run over ever since, on 1 June.

1878 Subway constructed to take Hammersmith & City tracks under the GWR main line between Royal Oak and Westbourne Park stations.

1879 Section opened by MDR from Turnham Green to Ealing Broadway station adjacent to that of the GWR, on 1 July.

1879 The St John's Wood branch opened a further extension from Swiss Cottage to West Hampstead on 1 July.

1880 Section from West Brompton to Putney Bridge opened by MDR on 1 March.

1880 Harrow-on-the-Hill was reached by Metropolitan Railway from West Hampstead on 2 August.

1880 Branch opened from Surrey Docks (ELR) to New Cross (LBSC).

Junctions underground were more complicated than outside by needing to avoid the uprights supporting the ceiling. This is the scene on the Metropolitan District Railway, with Mansion House station in the distance, in the mid-1870s.

Opening dates of stations, name changes and closures

Stations opened or first served

3.07.1871	Mansion House	MDR
30.10.1871	Royal Oak	H&CR
30.10.1871	Earl's Court	MDR *first site*
1.11.1871	Westbourne Park	H&CR *present site*
9.09.1874	Hammersmith	MDR
9.09.1874	North End (Fulham)	MDR
1.02.1875	Liverpool Street [GER]	MetR
12.07.1875	Bishopsgate	MetR
18.11.1876	Aldgate	MetR
1.06.1877	Gunnersbury [LSWR]	MDR
1.06.1877	Kew Gardens [LSWR]	MDR
1.06.1877	Richmond [LSWR]	MDR
1.06.1877	Shaftesbury Road [LSWR]	MDR
1.06.1877	Turnham Green [LSWR]	MDR
1.10.1877	Hammersmith (Grove Road) [LSWR]	MetR
1.02.1878	Earl's Court	MDR *present site*
30.06.1879	Finchley Road	MetR
30.06.1879	West Hampstead	MetR
1.07.1879	Acton Green	MDR
1.07.1879	Ealing Broadway	MDR
1.07.1879	Ealing Common	MDR
1.07.1879	Mill Hill Park	MDR
24.11.1879	Kilburn & Brondesbury	MetR
24.11.1879	Willesden Green	MetR
1.03.1880	Parsons Green	MDR
1.03.1880	Putney Bridge & Fulham	MDR
1.03.1880	Walham Green	MDR
2.08.1880	Harrow	MetR
2.08.1880	Kingsbury & Neasden	MetR

Station names changed

	from	*to*
10.04.1876	Wapping & Shadwell	Wapping
1.03.1877	North End (Fulham)	West Kensington
1880	Notting Hill (Ladbroke Grove)	Notting Hill & Ladbroke Grove

Stations last served by Underground trains

30.10.1871	Westbourne Park	MetR *first site*
11.07.1875	Liverpool Street [GER]	*first station*
31.01.1878	Earl's Court	MDR *first station*

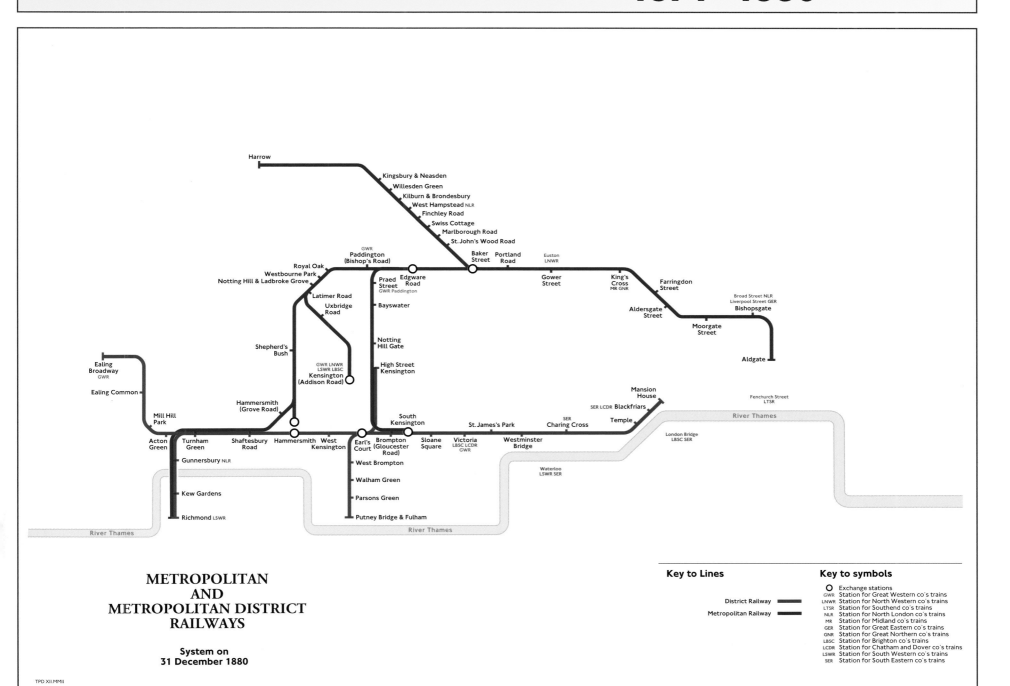

**METROPOLITAN
AND
METROPOLITAN DISTRICT
RAILWAYS**

**System on
31 December 1880**

Harrow

Kingsbury & Neasden
Willesden Green
Kilburn & Brondesbury
West Hampstead NLR
Finchley Road
Swiss Cottage
Marlborough Road
St. John's Wood Road

GWR
Paddington
(Bishop's Road)

Royal Oak
Westbourne Park
Notting Hill & Ladbroke Grove

Praed
Street
GWR Paddington

Edgware
Road

Baker
Street

Portland
Road

Euston
LNWR

Gower
Street

King's
Cross
MR GNR

Farringdon
Street

Broad Street NLR
Liverpool Street GER
Bishopsgate

Aldersgate
Street

Moorgate
Street

Latimer Road

Uxbridge
Road

Bayswater

Aldgate

Shepherd's
Bush

Notting
Hill Gate

GWR LNWR
LSWR LBSC
Kensington
(Addison Road)

High Street
Kensington

Ealing
Broadway
GWR

Ealing Common

Mansion
House

SER LCDR Blackfriars

Fenchurch Street
LTSR

Temple

River Thames

Mill Hill
Park

Hammersmith
(Grove Road)

South
Kensington

St. James's Park

SER
Charing Cross

Westminster
Bridge

Acton
Green

Turnham
Green

Shaftesbury
Road

Hammersmith

West
Kensington

Earl's
Court

Brompton
(Gloucester
Road)

Sloane
Square

Victoria
LBSC LCDR
GWR

London Bridge
LBSC SER

Gunnersbury NLR

West Brompton

Waterloo
LSWR SER

Kew Gardens

Walham Green

Parsons Green

Richmond LSWR

Putney Bridge & Fulham

River Thames

River Thames

River Thames

TPD XII.MMII

Key to Lines

District Railway

Metropolitan Railway

Key to symbols

○   Exchange stations
GWR   Station for Great Western co's trains
LNWR   Station for North Western co's trains
LTSR   Station for Southend co's trains
NLR   Station for North London co's trains
MR   Station for Midland co's trains
GER   Station for Great Eastern co's trains
GNR   Station for Great Northern co's trains
LBSC   Station for Brighton co's trains
LCDR   Station for Chatham and Dover co's trains
LSWR   Station for South Western co's trains
SER   Station for South Eastern co's trains

1881–1890

Principal developments of the decade

1883 District Railway started running a service between Mansion House, Ealing Broadway GWR and Windsor GWR, using its normal fleet of condensing tank locomotives and 4-wheeled carriages, from 1 March.

1883 District Railway opened line between Mill Hill Park and Hounslow (later re-named Hounslow Town) on 1 May.

1884 District Railway opened direct line to Hounslow Barracks on 21 July, leaving Hounslow Town as the terminus of a branch.

1886 Branch to Hounslow Town closed on 31 March.

1884 First Metropolitan and District services through Thames Tunnel to New Cross on 1 October.

1884 The final link to complete the Inner Circle opened between Mansion House and Aldgate on 6 October and was vested jointly with the Metropolitan District and Metropolitan railways. Intermediate stations were at Cannon Street, the Monument and Mark Lane (which replaced Tower of London). The clockwise service was run by Metropolitan Railway's trains, the anti-clockwise service by District Railway's trains with a few Metropolitan trains to maintain train mileage proportionate to the track mileage owned by each company.

1884 Mark Lane to Aldgate East, St Mary's (Whitechapel), and the connection with the East London Railway, owned jointly between the MDR and MetR, opened for through services on 6 October.

1885 Harrow to Pinner opened on 25 May.

1885 The District Railway's Windsor service suspended in favour of the faster and more comfortable GWR trains on 30 September.

1887 Pinner to Rickmansworth opened on 1 September.

1889 The LSWR builds its line from Putney Bridge to Wimbledon, which included the bridge at Putney over the Thames, and grants running powers to the MDR from 3 June.

1889 Rickmansworth to Chesham opened on 8 July.

1890 London's first deep level tube railway, the City & South London Railway, opened between King William Street and Stockwell on 18 December. Using electric locomotives hauling carriages, the trains ran through tunnels bored through London's clay and deep enough for stations to require lifts between platforms and ground level.

Because it was situated entirely on the private estate of the Duke of Buckingham, the Wotton Tramway did not require an Act of Parliament to permit its building. The tramway's original purpose was to carry goods and workers around the duke's estate. However it was later elevated in importance when the Metropolitan Railway took over the operation (but not ownership) of the line at the end of the nineteenth century. At one time there were plans, which were never fulfilled, to extend the terminus from Brill to Oxford.

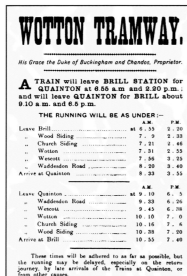

WOTTON TRAMWAY.

His Grace the Duke of Buckingham and Chandos, Proprietor.

A TRAIN will leave BRILL STATION for QUAINTON at 6.55 a.m and 2.20 p.m.; and will leave QUAINTON for BRILL about 9.10 a.m. and 6.5 p.m.

THE RUNNING WILL BE AS UNDER:—

	A.M.	P.M.
Leave Brill .... at	6.55	2.20
„ Wood Siding	7.9	2.33
„ Church Siding	7.21	2.46
„ Wotton	7.31	2.55
„ Wescott	7.56	3.25
„ Waddesdon Road	8.20	3.40
Arrive at Quainton	8.33	3.55

	A.M.	P.M.
Leave Quainton .... at	9.10	6.5
„ Waddesdon Road	9.33	6.26
„ Wescott	9.45	6.38
„ Wotton	10.10	7.0
„ Church Siding	10.16	7.6
„ Wood Siding	10.38	7.20
Arrive at Brill	10.55	7.40

These times will be adhered to as far as possible, but the running may be delayed, especially on the return journey, by late arrivals of the Trains at Quainton, or from other causes.

R. A. JONES, *Manager.*

Brill, October 1st, 1887.

DE FRAINE, PRINTER, " BUCKS HERALD " OFFICE, AYLESBURY.

Opening dates of stations, name changes and closures

Stations opened or first served by Underground trains

25.09.1882	Tower of London MDR MetR
1.03.1883	Castle Hill (Ealing Dean) [GWR] MDR
1.03.1883	Ealing Broadway [GWR] MDR
1.03.1883	Hanwell [GWR] MDR
1.03.1883	Hayes [GWR] MDR
1.03.1883	Langley [GWR] MDR
1.03.1883	Slough [GWR] MDR *first site*
1.03.1883	Southall [GWR] MDR
1.03.1883	West Drayton [GWR] MDR *first site*
1.03.1883	Windsor [GWR] MDR
1.05.1883	Boston Road MDR
1.05.1883	Hounslow MDR *original site*
1.05.1883	Osterley & Spring Grove MDR *first site*
1.05.1883	South Ealing MDR
21.07.1884	Hounslow Barracks MDR
9.08.1884	West Drayton [GWR] MDR *present site*
8.09.1884	Slough [GWR] MDR *present site*
1.10.1884	Deptford Road [ELR] MDR MetR
1.10.1884	New Cross LBSC [ELR] MDR
1.10.1884	New Cross SER [ELR] MetR
1.10.1884	Rotherhithe [ELR] MDR MetR
1.10.1884	St.Mary's MDR MetR
1.10.1884	Shadwell [ELR] MDR MetR
1.10.1884	Wapping [ELR] MDR MetR
6.10.1884	Aldgate East MDR MetR *first site*
6.10.1884	Cannon Street MDR MetR
6.10.1884	Eastcheap MDR MetR
6.10.1884	Mark Lane MDR MetR
6.10.1884	Whitechapel (Mile End) MDR
25.05.1885	Pinner MetR
1.04.1886	Heston-Hounslow MDR
1.09.1887	Northwood MetR
1.09.1887	Rickmansworth MetR
3.06.1889	East Putney MDR
3.06.1889	Southfields MDR
3.06.1889	Wimbledon [LSWR] MDR
3.06.1889	Wimbledon Park [LSWR] MDR
8.07.1889	Chesham MetR
8.07.1889	Chalfont Road MetR
8.07.1889	Chorley Wood MetR
18.12.1890	Borough C&SLR
18.12.1890	Elephant & Castle C&SLR
18.12.1890	Kennington C&SLR
18.12.1890	King William Street C&SLR
18.12.1890	The Oval C&SLR
18.12.1890	Stockwell C&SLR

Station names changed

	from	to
1.05.1882	Torrington Park, Woodside [GNR]	Woodside Park [GNR]
21.07.1884	Hounslow	Hounslow Town
1.11.1884	Eastcheap	The Monument
11.09.1885	Finchley Road	Finchley Road (South Hampstead)
1886	Ealing Common	Ealing Common & West Acton
1.02.1887	East End, Finchley	East Finchley
03.1887	Acton Green	Chiswick Park & Acton Green
1.03.1888	Shaftesbury Road	Ravenscourt Park

Stations last served by Underground trains

8.08.1884	West Drayton MDR *first station*
7.09.1884	Slough [GWR] MDR *first station*
12.10.1884	Tower of London MDR MetR
30.09.1885	Castle Hill (Ealing Dean) [GWR] MDR
30.09.1885	Ealing Broadway [GWR]) MDR
30.09.1885	Hanwell [GWR] MDR
30.09.1885	Hayes [GWR] MDR
30.09.1885	Langley [GWR] MDR
30.09.1885	Slough [GWR] MDR *second station*
30.09.1885	Southall [GWR] MDR
30.09.1885	West Drayton [GWR] MDR *second station*
30.09.1885	Windsor [GWR] MDR
31.3.1886	Hounslow Town MDR

When the District Railway worked its own system it had 24 engines built in 1871, which were similar to those already in use by the Metropolitan Railway. It ordered more in 1876, 1880, 1883, 1884 and 1886, bringing the total to 54, to go with its 4-wheeled compartment coaches, all of which lasted until the end of steam on the District early in the twentieth century. This type of train also provided the short-lived service from Mansion House to Windsor which ran from 1 March 1883 to 30 September 1885, but was no match for the GWR 8-wheeled carriages running smoothly on broad gauge tracks behind powerful engines.

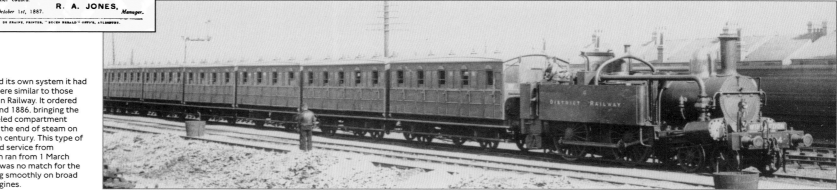

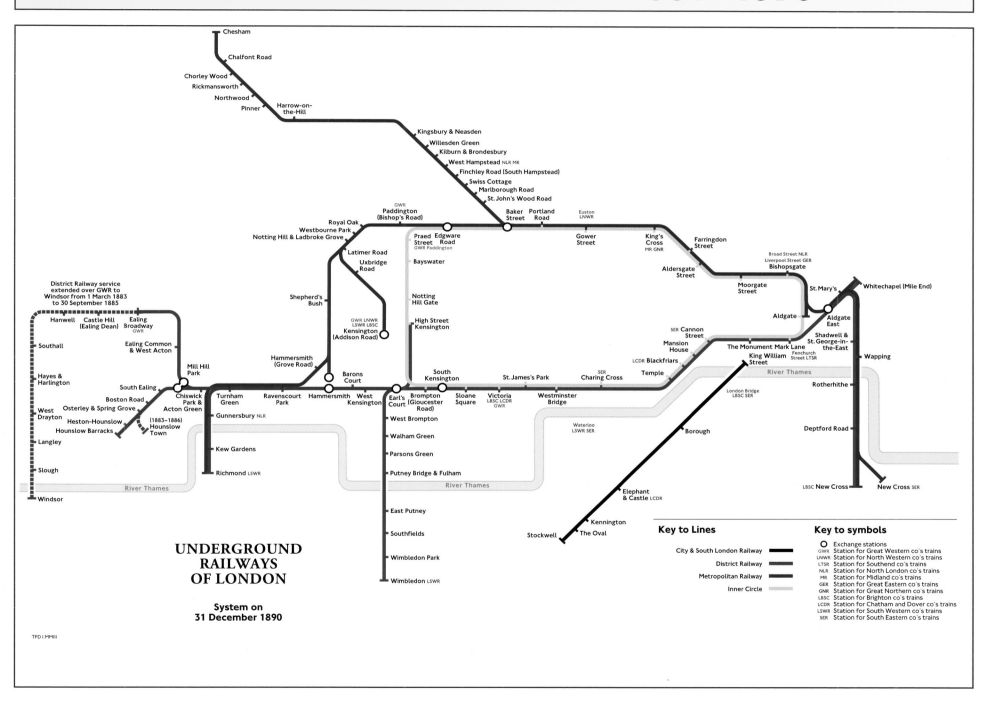

Chesham
Chalfont Road
Chorley Wood
Rickmansworth
Northwood
Pinner
Harrow-on-the-Hill
Kingsbury & Neasden
Willesden Green
Kilburn & Brondesbury
West Hampstead NLR MR
Finchley Road (South Hampstead)
Swiss Cottage
Marlborough Road
St. John's Wood Road

GWR
Paddington (Bishop's Road)
Royal Oak
Westbourne Park
Notting Hill & Ladbroke Grove
Latimer Road
Uxbridge Road
Shepherd's Bush

Praed Street
Edgware Road
GWR Paddington
Bayswater
Notting Hill Gate
High Street Kensington

Baker Street
Portland Road
Euston LNWR
Gower Street
King's Cross MR GNR
Farringdon Street

Broad Street NLR
Liverpool Street GER
Bishopsgate
Aldersgate Street
Moorgate Street
St. Mary's
Aldgate
Whitechapel (Mile End)
Aldgate East
Shadwell & St. George-in-the-East
Wapping

District Railway service extended over GWR to Windsor from 1 March 1883 to 30 September 1885

Hanwell
Castle Hill (Ealing Dean)
Ealing Broadway GWR
Southall
Ealing Common & West Acton
GWR LNWR LSWR LBSC
Kensington (Addison Road)

Hayes & Harlington
Mill Hill Park
Hammersmith (Grove Road)

West Drayton
South Ealing
Boston Road
Osterley & Spring Grove
Heston-Hounslow
Hounslow Barracks

Chiswick Park & Acton Green
(1883–1886) Hounslow Town
Gunnersbury NLR
Turnham Green
Ravenscourt Park
Hammersmith
West Kensington
Barons Court
Earl's Court
Brompton (Gloucester Road)
Sloane Square
Victoria LBSC LCDR GWR
Westminster Bridge

SER Cannon Street
Mansion House
The Monument   Mark Lane
Fenchurch Street LTSR
LCDR Blackfriars
King William Street
Temple
St. James's Park
SER Charing Cross
South Kensington

Langley
Slough
Windsor

Kew Gardens
Richmond LSWR

West Brompton
Walham Green
Parsons Green
Putney Bridge & Fulham

East Putney
Southfields
Wimbledon Park
Wimbledon LSWR

Waterloo LSWR SER
Borough
Elephant & Castle LCDR
Kennington
The Oval
Stockwell

London Bridge LBSC SER
River Thames
Rotherhithe
Deptford Road
LBSC New Cross
New Cross SER

River Thames

UNDERGROUND RAILWAYS OF LONDON

System on 31 December 1890

TPD I.MMIII

Key to Lines

City & South London Railway ▬▬▬
District Railway ▬▬▬
Metropolitan Railway ▬▬▬
Inner Circle ▬▬▬

Key to symbols

○ Exchange stations
GWR Station for Great Western co's trains
LNWR Station for North Western co's trains
LTSR Station for Southend co's trains
NLR Station for North London co's trains
MR Station for Midland co's trains
GER Station for Great Eastern co's trains
GNR Station for Great Northern co's trains
LBSC Station for Brighton co's trains
LCDR Station for Chatham and Dover co's trains
LSWR Station for South Western co's trains
SER Station for South Eastern co's trains

Principal developments of the decade

Central London Railway

1900 Opening of Central London Railway between Shepherd's Bush and Bank, with intermediate stations at Holland Park, Notting Hill Gate, Queen's Road, Lancaster Gate, Marble Arch, Oxford Circus, Tottenham Court Road, British Museum, Chancery Lane and Post Office, on 30 July. Bond Street opened on 24 September.

City & South London Railway

1900 City & South London Railway opened the section between Borough and Moorgate Street, with stations at London Bridge and Bank and closed their original City terminus at King William Street, on 25 February.

1900 Extension from Stockwell to Clapham Common with an intermediate station at Clapham Road (now Clapham North) opened on 3 June.

Metropolitan Railway

1891 Aylesbury & Buckingham Railway absorbed by Metropolitan Railway, 1 July.

1892 The line opened between Chalfont Road and Aylesbury South Junction, with intermediate stations at Amersham, Great Missenden, Wendover and Stoke Mandeville, on 1 September.

1894 Aylesbury South Junction connected to North Junction and to the Metropolitan Railway's newly absorbed Aylesbury to Verney Junction section, on 1 January.

1899 Working of the Quainton Road to Brill Oxford & Aylesbury Tramroad was taken over by the Metropolitan Railway on 1 December. Ownership of the trackbed remained with the Trustees of the late Earl Temple's Estate.

Metropolitan and District Railways

1900 While both railways accept the need and urgency to electrify the Inner Circle line, neither could agree as to the system to be employed. The Metropolitan Railway favoured high voltage 3-phase alternating current, collected from two overhead wires. The District Railway wished to proceed with the direct current third rail system, already used by the City & South London and Central London tubes, the Liverpool Overhead Railway, numerous American cities and by metropolitan railways in Berlin, Paris and Budapest (home of Ganz & Co, the manufacturers of the Metropolitan Railway's preferred 3-phase equipment). A Board of Trade arbitration commission, which was set up on 29 October, reported on 15 November in favour of the direct current system proposed by the District Railway.

Waterloo & City Railway

1898 Waterloo & City Railway opened and, being worked by the London & South Western Railway, gave them a rail connection across the River Thames to the financial heart of London, on 8 August.

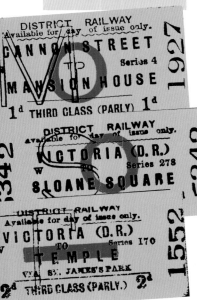

Ticket security Is not new. At the end of the nineteenth century the District and Metropolitan railways were printing various devices on their tickets to help ease checking. On Inner Circle tickets the red 'O' in the centre referred to clockwise travel on the Outer rail. Conversely, a red 'I' indicated anti-clockwise journeys on the Inner rail. Large outline letters were intended to help ticket collectors at barriers identify their own stations.

The Central London Railway opened using electric locomotives hauling trains of carriages, as had the City & South London Railway when it opened ten years earlier. But the CLR's engines were heavier and more powerful, causing vibration to the driver as well as to occupants of buildings above the line. It can be seen here how the driver was accommodated within the massive steel frames of the engine.

Opening dates of stations, name changes and closures

Stations opened or first served by Underground trains

1.07.1891	Grandborough Road	MetR *opened by A&BR 23.09.1868*
1.07.1891	Quainton Road	MetR *opened by A&BR 23.09.1868*
1.07.1891	Verney Junction	MetR *opened by A&BR 23.09.1868*
1.07.1891	Winslow Road	MetR *opened by A&BR 23.09.1868*
1.09.1892	Amersham	MetR
1.09.1892	Aylesbury	MetR *first site*
1.09.1892	Great Missenden	MetR
1.09.1892	Stoke Mandeville	MetR
1.09.1892	Wendover	MetR
1.01.1894	Aylesbury	MetR *present site*
12.05.1894	Wembley Park	MetR
30.11.1896	Quainton Road	MetR *present site*
1.01.1897	Waddesdon Manor	MetR
8.08.1898	City [W&CR]	
8.08.1898	Waterloo [W&CR]	
1.12.1899	Brill [O&AT]	MetR *opened by WT 06.1872*
1.12.1899	Waddesdon Road [O&AT]	MetR *opened by WT 1.04.1871*
1.12.1899	Westcott [O&AT]	MetR *opened by WT 1.04.1871*
1.12.1899	Wood Siding [O&AT]	MetR *opened by WT 06.1871*
1.12.1899	Wotton [O&AT]	MetR *opened by WT 1.04.1871*
25.02.1900	Bank	C&SLR
25.02.1900	London Bridge	C&SLR
25.02.1900	Moorgate Street	C&SLR
3.06.1900	Clapham Common	C&SLR
3.06.1900	Clapham Road	C&SLR
30.07.1900	Bank	CLR
30.07.1900	British Museum	CLR
30.07.1900	Chancery Lane	CLR
30.07.1900	Holland Park	CLR
30.07.1900	Lancaster Gate	CLR
30.07.1900	Marble Arch	CLR
30.07.1900	Notting Hill Gate	CLR
30.07.1900	Oxford Circus	CLR
30.07.1900	Post Office	CLR
30.07.1900	Queen's Road	CLR
30.07.1900	Shepherd's Bush	CLR
30.07.1900	Tottenham Court Road	CLR
24.09.1900	Bond Street	CLR

Station names changed

	from	to
1894	The Oval	Oval
1.06.1894	Harrow	Harrow-on-the-Hill
1.06.1894	Willesden Green & Cricklewood	Willesden Green
1.07.1900	Shadwell-in-the-East	Shadwell & St.George

Stations last served by Underground trains

31.12.1893	Aylesbury	*first site*
29.11.1896	Quainton Road	*first site*
24.02.1900	King William Street	C&SLR

C. L. R. Twopenny Tube. The Train.

This train run about 90 feet under ground, very nice travels too they be.

1340.

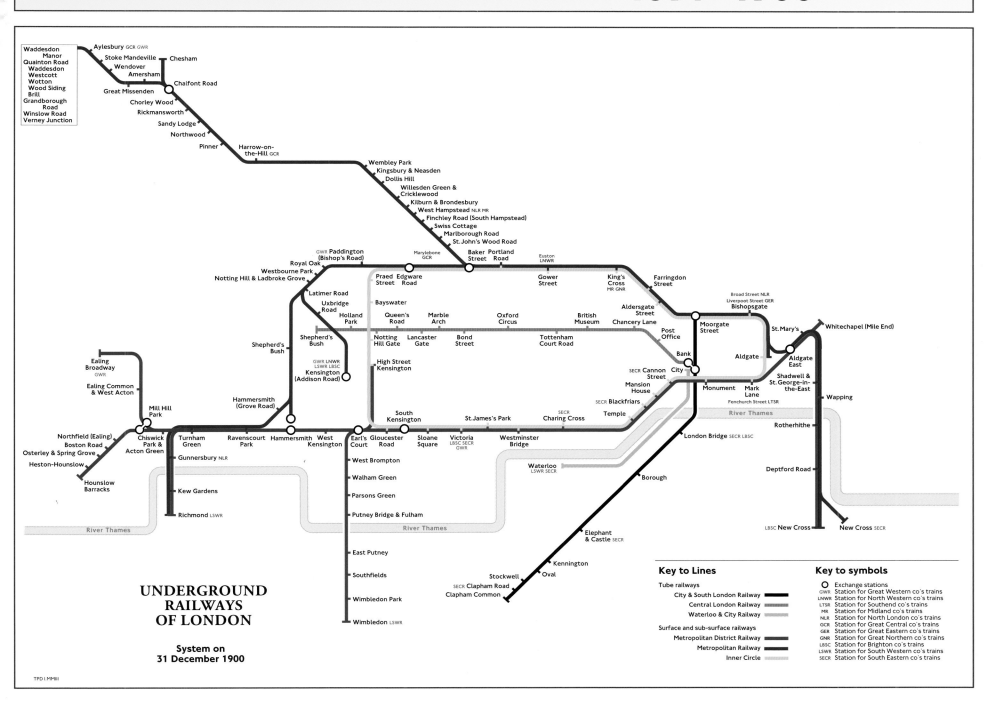

UNDERGROUND RAILWAYS OF LONDON

System on 31 December 1900

Key to Lines

Tube railways

City & South London Railway

Central London Railway

Waterloo & City Railway

Surface and sub-surface railways

Metropolitan District Railway

Metropolitan Railway

Inner Circle

Key to symbols

O Exchange stations
GWR Station for Great Western co's trains
LNWR Station for North Western co's trains
LTSR Station for Southend co's trains
MR Station for Midland co's trains
NLR Station for North London co's trains
GCR Station for Great Central co's trains
GER Station for Great Eastern co's trains
GNR Station for Great Northern co's trains
LBSC Station for Brighton co's trains
LSWR Station for South Western co's trains
SECR Station for South Eastern co's trains

TPD I.MMIII

UNDERGROUND.
DISTRICT RAILWAY.
Issued subject to the Companies' Bye Laws, Rules, Regulations and advertised Conditions.
Mansion House
S.76 TO S.76
VICTORIA
or any intermediate Station.
ORDINARY CAR (3rd Class) FARE 2d.
Available on day of issue only.
8779 8779

London & South Western Ry.
RICHMOND NEW to
KEW GARDENS
840
Richmond New Kew Gardens	Richmond New Kew Gardens
THIRD CLASS	(S.152) See over	THIRD CLASS
Fare 1d	Fare 1d

1 January   31 December

1901–1910

Principal developments of the decade

UNDERGROUND

LONDON . . .

WHAT TO SEE & HOW TO SEE IT. . .

THE EXCURSIONISTS' GUIDE WITH MAP. .

TRAVEL AT YOUR EASE FROM ANYWHERE to EVERYWHERE of INTEREST by "UNDERGROUND."

Baker Street & Waterloo Railway

1906 Opening of line, Baker Street to Kennington Road, on 10 March.

1906 Extension southwards from Kennington Road to Elephant & Castle opened on 5 July.

1907 Baker Street to Great Central opened on 27 March.

1907 Great Central to Edgware Road opened on 15 June.

Central London Railway

1908 Shepherd's Bush to Wood Lane extension opened on 14 May.

Charing Cross, Euston & Hampstead Railway

1907 Opening of line, Strand to Golders Green and Highgate (now Archway), on 22 June.

City & South London Railway

1907 Moorgate Street to Euston opened on 12 May.

Great Northern & City Railway

1904 Opening of line on 14 February.

Great Northern, Piccadilly & Brompton Railway

1906 Opening of line, Hammersmith to Finsbury Park, on 15 December.

1907 Holborn to Strand branch opened on 30 November.

Metropolitan District Railway

1902 Whitechapel & Bow Railway opened, extending District services eastward, on 2 June.

1903 Branch to Hounslow Town re-opened on 1 March.

1903 First electric trains from Ealing to South Harrow from 23 June.

1905 Electric trains replaced steam, Ealing Broadway to Whitechapel, from 1 June.

1905 Electric trains replaced steam, Hounslow to South Acton, from 13 June.

1905 Spur from Hounslow Town branch in the direction of Hounslow Barracks opened on 13 June.

1909 Hounslow Town and its branch closed on 1 May.

Metropolitan Railway

1904 Harrow to Uxbridge opened on 4 July.

1905 Steam replaced by electric service, Baker Street to Uxbridge, from 1 January.

1905 First stage of Inner Circle (Metropolitan and District) electrification brought into use on 1 July.

1906 Harrow-on-the-Hill to Verney Junction line via Aylesbury, and Chesham branch, leased to Metropolitan & Great Central Joint Committee for the use of Metropolitan Railway and Great Central Railway services from 2 April.

1910 Pullman cars introduced on business and evening 'theatre' trains between Verney Junction, Aylesbury, Chesham and Baker Street and the City on 1 June.

1905 Electric trains replaced steam, Putney Bridge to High Street Kensington, from 23 June.

1905 Electric trains replaced steam over LSWR lines, between Richmond and Turnham Green, from 18 July.

1905 Electric traction inaugurated between Whitechapel and East Ham, partly over LTSR, from 20 August.

1905 Electric trains commenced running over LSWR line between Putney Bridge and Wimbledon from 27 August.

1908 Electric traction inaugurated, East Ham to Barking over LTSR, from 1 April.

Waterloo & City Railway

1907 Absorbed by LSWR on 1 January.

PRINCIPAL AMALGAMATIONS

1902 Formation of the Underground Electric Railways Company of London Ltd, by Mr C. T. Yerkes, on 9 April.

1908 Tube railways and Metropolitan and District agree on common publicity use of the word UNDERGROUND.

1910 The Bakerloo, Hampstead and Piccadilly tubes amalgamate as the London Electric Railway as a subsidiary of the Underground Electric Railways on 1 July.

Opening dates of stations, name changes and closures

Stations opened or first served by Underground trains

17.11.1901	Angel C&SLR
17.11.1901	City Road C&SLR
17.11.1901	Old Street C&SLR
2.06.1902	Barking [LTSR] MDR
2.06.1902	Bromley [LTSR] MDR
2.06.1902	Dagenham [LTSR] MDR
2.06.1902	East Ham [LTSR] MDR
2.06.1902	Hornchurch [LTSR] MDR
2.06.1902	Mile End MDR
2.06.1902	Plaistow [LTSR] MDR
2.06.1902	Upton Park [LTSR] MDR
2.06.1902	Upminster [LTSR] MDR
2.06.1902	West Ham [LTSR] MDR
2.06.1902	Whitechapel MDR re-opened
1.03.1903	Hounslow Town MDR re-opened
23.06.1903	North Ealing MDR
23.06.1903	Park Royal & Twyford Abbey MDR first site
28.06.1903	Perivale-Alperton MDR
28.06.1903	South Harrow MDR first site
28.06.1903	Sudbury Hill MDR
28.06.1903	Sudbury Town MDR
14.02.1904	Drayton Park GN&CR
14.02.1904	Essex Road GN&CR
14.02.1904	Finsbury Park GN&CR
14.02.1904	Moorgate GN&CR
14.02.1904	Old Street GN&CR
28.06.1904	Highbury GN&CR
4.07.1904	Uxbridge MetR
4.07.1904	Ruislip MetR
13.06.1905	South Acton MDR
25.09.1905	Ickenham MetR
9.10.1905	Barons Court MDR
10.03.1906	Baker Street BS&WR
10.03.1906	Embankment BS&WR
10.03.1906	Kennington Road BS&WR
10.03.1906	Oxford Circus BS&WR
10.03.1906	Piccadilly Circus BS&WR
10.03.1906	Regent's Park BS&WR
10.03.1906	Trafalgar Square BS&WR
10.03.1906	Waterloo BS&WR
26.05.1906	Eastcote MetR
26.05.1906	Rayners Lane MetR
5.08.1906	Elephant & Castle BS&WR
15.12.1906	Barons Court GNP&BR
15.12.1906	Brompton Road GNP&BR
15.12.1906	Caledonian Road GNP&BR
15.12.1906	Dover Street GNP&BR
15.12.1906	Earl's Court GNP&BR
15.12.1906	Finsbury Park GNP&BR
15.12.1906	Gillespie Road GNP&BR
15.12.1906	Gloucester Road GNP&BR
15.12.1906	Hammersmith GNP&BR
15.12.1906	Holborn GNP&BR
15.12.1906	Holloway Road GNP&BR
15.12.1906	Hyde Park Corner GNP&BR
15.12.1906	King's Cross GNP&BR
15.12.1906	Knightsbridge GNP&BR
15.12.1906	Leicester Square GNP&BR
15.12.1906	Piccadilly Circus GNP&BR
15.12.1906	Russell Square GNP&BR
15.12.1906	York Road GNP&BR
8.01.1907	South Kensington GNP&BR
15.03.1907	Down Street GNP&BR
27.03.1907	Great Central BS&WR
11.04.1907	Covent Garden GNP&BR
12.05.1907	Euston C&SLR
12.05.1907	King's Cross for St.Pancras C&SLR
15.06.1907	Edgware Road BS&WR
22.06.1907	Belsize Park CCE&HR
22.06.1907	Camden Town CCE&HR
22.06.1907	Chalk Farm CCE&HR
22.06.1907	Charing Cross CCE&HR
22.06.1907	Euston CCE&HR
22.06.1907	Euston Road CCE&HR
22.06.1907	Golders Green CCE&HR
22.06.1907	Hampstead CCE&HR
22.06.1907	Highgate CCE&HR
22.06.1907	Leicester Square CCE&HR
22.06.1907	Kentish Town CCE&HR
22.06.1907	Mornington Crescent CCE&HR
22.06.1907	Oxford Street CCE&HR
22.06.1907	South Kentish Town CCE&HR
22.06.1907	Tottenham Court Road CCE&HR
22.06.1907	Tufnell Park CCE&HR
30.11.1907	Strand GNP&BR
16.04.1908	Northfields (Ealing) MDR
1.05.1908	Wood Lane (Exhibition) H&CR
14.05.1908	Wood Lane CLR
21.05.1908	Preston Road MetR
2.05.1909	Hounslow Town MDR on main line
1.10.1909	Dollis Hill MetR
9.05.1910	Sandy Lodge MetR

Station names changed

Date	from	to
13.11.1901	Whitechapel (Mile End)	Whitechapel
1.09.1902	Putney Bridge & Hurlingham	Putney Bridge & Fulham
5.06.1906	Kennington Road	Westminster Bridge Road
1907	Westminster Bridge	Westminster
1907	Brompton (Gloucester Road)	Gloucester Road
9.03.1908	Oxford Street	Tottenham Court Road
9.03.1908	Tottenham Court Road	Goodge Street
7.06.1908	Euston Road	Warren Street
1.11.1909	Gower Street	Euston Square
1.11.1909	Bishopsgate	Liverpool Street
1.01.1910	Kingsbury & Neasden	Neasden & Kingsbury
1.03.1910	Chiswick Park & Acton Green	Chiswick Park
1.03.1910	Ealing Common & West Acton	Ealing Common
1.03.1910	Mill Hill Park	Acton Town
7.10.1910	Perivale-Alperton	Alperton
1.11.1910	Aldersgate Street	Aldersgate

Stations last served by Underground trains

30.09.1905	Barking [LT&SR] MDR
30.09.1905	Dagenham [LT&SR] MDR
30.09.1905	Hornchurch [LT&SR] MDR
30.09.1905	Upminster [LT&SR] MDR
2.12.1906	Deptford Road [ELR] MDR MetR
2.12.1906	New Cross [ELR] MDR MetR
2.12.1906	Rotherhithe [ELR] MDR MetR
2.12.1906	Shadwell & St.George-in-the-East [ELR] MDR MetR
2.12.1906	Wapping [ELR] MDR MetR
31.12.1906	Hammersmith (Grove Road) [LSWR] MetR closed 1916
1.05.1909	Hounslow Town MDR branch terminal

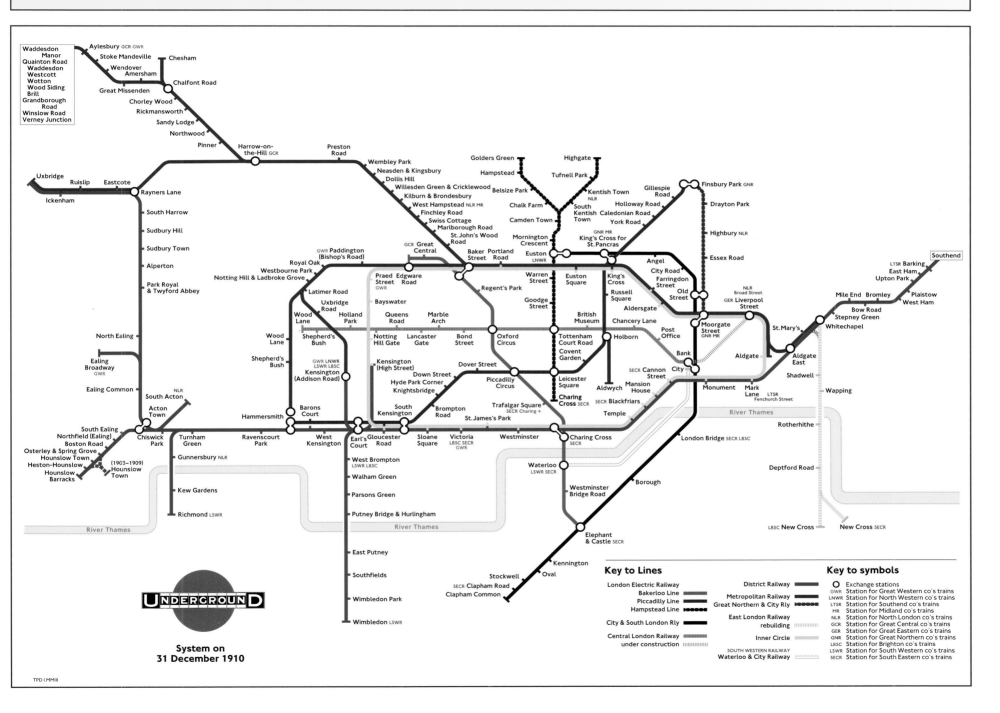

Waddesdon Manor
Quainton Road
Waddesdon
Westcott
Wotton
Wood Siding
Brill
Grandborough Road
Winslow Road
Verney Junction

Aylesbury GCR GWR
Stoke Mandeville
Wendover
Amersham
Chesham
Great Missenden
Chalfont Road
Chorley Wood
Rickmansworth
Sandy Lodge
Northwood
Pinner
Harrow-on-the-Hill GCR
Preston Road
Wembley Park
Neasden & Kingsbury
Dollis Hill
Willesden Green & Cricklewood
Kilburn & Brondesbury
West Hampstead NLR MR
Finchley Road
Swiss Cottage
Marlborough Road
St. John's Wood Road
Baker Street
Portland Road

Uxbridge
Ruislip
Eastcote
Ickenham
Rayners Lane
South Harrow
Sudbury Hill
Sudbury Town
Alperton
Park Royal & Twyford Abbey
North Ealing
Ealing Broadway GWR
Ealing Common
South Acton NLR
Acton Town
South Ealing
Northfield (Ealing)
Boston Road
Osterley & Spring Grove
Hounslow Town
Heston-Hounslow
Hounslow Barracks
(1903–1909) Hounslow Town
Chiswick Park
Turnham Green
Gunnersbury NLR
Ravenscourt Park
Kew Gardens
Richmond LSWR

Golders Green
Hampstead
Highgate
Tufnell Park
Belsize Park
Chalk Farm
Camden Town
Kentish Town NLR
South Kentish Town
Mornington Crescent
Euston
LNWR
Gillespie Road
Holloway Road
Caledonian Road
York Road
King's Cross for St. Pancras
GNR MR
Finsbury Park GNR
Drayton Park
Highbury NLR
Essex Road
Angel

GWR Paddington (Bishop's Road)
Royal Oak
Westbourne Park
Notting Hill & Ladbroke Grove
Latimer Road
Uxbridge Road
Wood Lane
Holland Park
Shepherd's Bush
Shepherd's Bush
GWR LNWR LSWR LBSC
Kensington (Addison Road)
Barons Court
Hammersmith
West Kensington
GCR Great Central
Praed Street GWR
Edgware Road
Bayswater
Queens Road
Notting Hill Gate
Kensington (High Street)
Down Street
Hyde Park Corner
Knightsbridge
South Kensington
Gloucester Road
Earl's Court
Warren Street
Euston Square
King's Cross
Russell Square
Regent's Park
Goodge Street
British Museum
Marble Arch
Lancaster Gate
Bond Street
Oxford Circus
Tottenham Court Road
Covent Garden
Dover Street
Piccadilly Circus
Leicester Square
Charing Cross SECR
Aldwych
Trafalgar Square
SECR Charing +
St. James's Park
Brompton Road
City Road
Farringdon Street
Old Street
Chancery Lane
Post Office
Aldersgate
Holborn
Bank
Mansion House
SECR Cannon Street
City
Monument
SECR Blackfriars
Temple
Moorgate Street GNR MR
NLR Broad Street
GER Liverpool Street
Aldgate
Mark Lane
LTSR Fenchurch Street
Aldgate East
St. Mary's
Shadwell

Victoria LBSC SECR GWR
Sloane Square
Westminster
Charing Cross SECR
Waterloo LSWR SECR
Westminster Bridge Road
Borough
London Bridge SECR LBSC
Elephant & Castle SECR
Kennington
Oval
Stockwell
SECR Clapham Road
Clapham Common

West Brompton LSWR LBSC
Walham Green
Parsons Green
Putney Bridge & Hurlingham
East Putney
Southfields
Wimbledon Park
Wimbledon LSWR

Wapping
Rotherhithe
Deptford Road
LBSC New Cross
New Cross SECR
River Thames
River Thames

LTSR Barking
East Ham
Upton Park
Mile End
Bow Road
Stepney Green
Whitechapel
Plaistow
West Ham
Southend

UNDERGROUND

System on 31 December 1910

TPD I.MMIII

Key to Lines

London Electric Railway
Bakerloo Line
Piccadilly Line
Hampstead Line

City & South London Rly

Central London Railway
under construction

District Railway
Metropolitan Railway
Great Northern & City Rly

East London Railway
rebuilding

Inner Circle

SOUTH WESTERN RAILWAY
Waterloo & City Railway

Key to symbols

O   Exchange stations
GWR   Station for Great Western co's trains
LNWR   Station for North Western co's trains
LTSR   Station for Southend co's trains
MR   Station for Midland co's trains
NLR   Station for North London co's trains
GCR   Station for Great Central co's trains
GER   Station for Great Eastern co's trains
GNR   Station for Great Northern co's trains
LBSC   Station for Brighton co's trains
LSWR   Station for South Western co's trains
SECR   Station for South Eastern co's trains

13

1911–1920

Principal developments of the decade

Bakerloo Line

1913 Extension from Edgware Road to Paddington opened on 1 December.

1915 Extension from Paddington to Queen's Park opened on 11 February.

1917 Through running over London & North Western Railway tracks from Queen's Park to Watford commenced on 16 April.

Central London Railway

1912 Bank to Liverpool Street opened on 28 July.

1920 Inauguration of through running to Ealing Broadway over the GWR-built Ealing & Shepherd's Bush Railway on 3 August.

East London Railway

1913 Inauguration of electric trains, Shoreditch to New Cross LBSCR and New Cross SECR, on 31 March.

Great Northern & City Railway

1913 Absorbed by Metropolitan Railway on 1 June, whilst remaining physically unconnected.

Metropolitan District Railway

1910 Electric train service extended from South Harrow to Rayners Lane, sharing Metropolitan Railway tracks onwards to Uxbridge, from 1 March.

1911 First escalator on a London tube railway came into use at Earl's Court on 4 October.

PASS DOWN THE PLATFORM

There are four, five, or six cars to a train. There are two gates to a car, and sometimes three. Two passengers cannot get through the same gate at the same time, but they can get through different gates at the same time. Even loading means quicker loading and in comfort.

UNDERGROUND

ELECTRIC RAILWAY HOUSE,
BROADWAY, WESTMINSTER, S.W.1

Opening dates of stations, name changes and closures

Stations opened or first served by Underground trains

1.02.1912	Stamford Brook	MDR
28.07.1912	Liverpool Street	CLR
5.08.1912	Ruislip Manor	MetR
31.03.1913	New Cross [LBSC]	ELR MetR *re-opened*
31.03.1913	New Cross [SECR]	ELR MetR *re-opened*
31.03.1913	Shadwell & St.George-in-the-East	ELR MetR
31.03.1913	Shoreditch	ELR MetR *re-opened*
31.03.1913	Surrey Docks	ELR MetR *re-opened*
31.03.1913	Wapping	ELR MetR *re-opened*
31.03.1913	Whitechapel	ELR *re-opened*
17.11.1913	West Harrow	MetR
1.12.1913	Paddington	BS&WR
1.04.1914	Goldhawk Road	MetR
1.04.1914	Shepherd's Bush	H&CR *present site*
6.04.1914	Charing Cross (Embankment)	CCE&HR
31.01.1915	Warwick Avenue	BS&WR
31.01.1915	Kilburn Park	BS&WR
11.02.1915	Queen's Park	BS&WR-LNWR JOINT
22.03.1915	North Harrow	MetR
10.05.1915	Willesden Junction	BS&WR-LNWR JOINT
6.06.1915	Maida Vale	BS&WR
1.10.1916	Kensal Green	BS&WR
16.04.1917	Harlesden	BS&WR-LNWR JOINT
16.04.1917	Wembley for Sudbury	BS&WR-LNWR JOINT
16.04.1917	North Wembley	BS&WR-LNWR JOINT
16.04.1917	Kenton	BS&WR-LNWR JOINT
16.04.1917	Harrow & Wealdstone	BS&WR-LNWR JOINT
16.04.1917	Headstone Lane	BS&WR-LNWR JOINT
16.04.1917	Pinner & Hatch End	BS&WR-LNWR JOINT
16.04.1917	Bushey & Oxhey	BS&WR-LNWT JOINT
16.04.1917	Watford High Street	BS&WR-LNWR JOINT
16.04.1917	Watford Junction	BS&WR-LNWR JOINT
1.08.1917	Stonebridge Park	BS&WR-LNWR JOINT *re-opened*
1.04.1919	Ruislip Manor	MetR *re-opened*
5.05.1919	Carpenders Park	BS&WR-LNWR JOINT *first site*
3.08.1920	Ealing Broadway	CLR
3.08.1920	East Acton	CLR

Station names changed

Date	from	to
17.07.1911	Deptford Road	Surrey Docks
11.12.1911	Northfield (Ealing)	Northfields & Little Ealing
11.12.1911	Boston Road	Boston Manor
c1914	Finchley Road (South Hampstead)	Finchley Road
6.04.1914	Embankment [BS&WR]	Charing Cross (Embankment)
6.04.1914	Charing Cross [CCE&HR]	Charing Cross (Strand)
9.05.1915	Charing Cross (Embankment)	Charing Cross [BS&WR and CCE&HR]
9.05.1915	Charing Cross (Strand)	Strand [CCE&HR]
9.05.1915	Strand [GNP&BR]	Aldwych
1.11.1915	Chalfont Road	Chalfont & Latimer
1.11.1915	Chorley Wood	Chorley Wood & Chenies
1.03.1917	Portland Road	Great Portland Street
15.04.1917	Great Central	Marylebone
15.04.1917	Westminster Bridge Road	Lambeth (North)
1918	Shadwell & St.George-in-the-East	Shadwell
1.06.1919	Notting Hill & Ladbroke Grove	Ladbroke Grove (North Kensington)
5.05.1920	Wood Lane (Exhibition)	Wood Lane (White City)
6.10.1920	Grandborough Road	Granborough Road

Stations last served by Underground trains

31.03.1914	Shepherd's Bush	MetR *first site*
11.02.1917	Ruislip Manor	MetR *temporary closure*

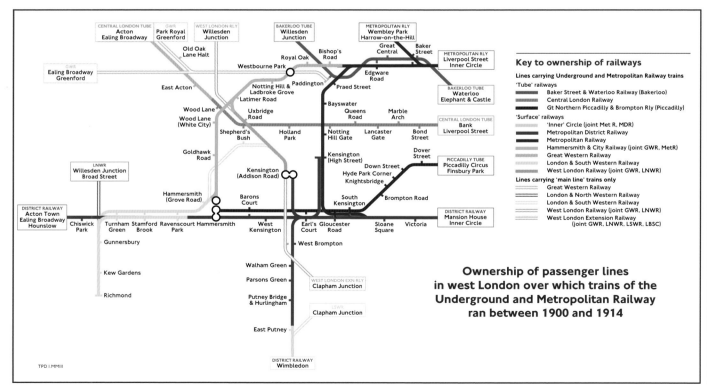

Key to ownership of railways

Lines carrying Underground and Metropolitan Railway trains

'Tube' railways
- Baker Street & Waterloo Railway (Bakerloo)
- Central London Railway
- Gt Northern Piccadilly & Brompton Rly (Piccadilly)

'Surface' railways
- 'Inner' Circle (joint Met R, MDR)
- Metropolitan District Railway
- Metropolitan Railway
- Hammersmith & City Railway (joint GWR, MetR)
- Great Western Railway
- London & South Western Railway
- West London Railway (joint GWR, LNWR)

Lines carrying 'main line' trains only
- Great Western Railway
- London & North Western Railway
- London & South Western Railway
- West London Railway (joint GWR, LNWR)
- West London Extension Railway (joint GWR, LNWR, LSWR, LBSC)

Ownership of passenger lines in west London over which trains of the Underground and Metropolitan Railway ran between 1900 and 1914

TPD I.MMIII

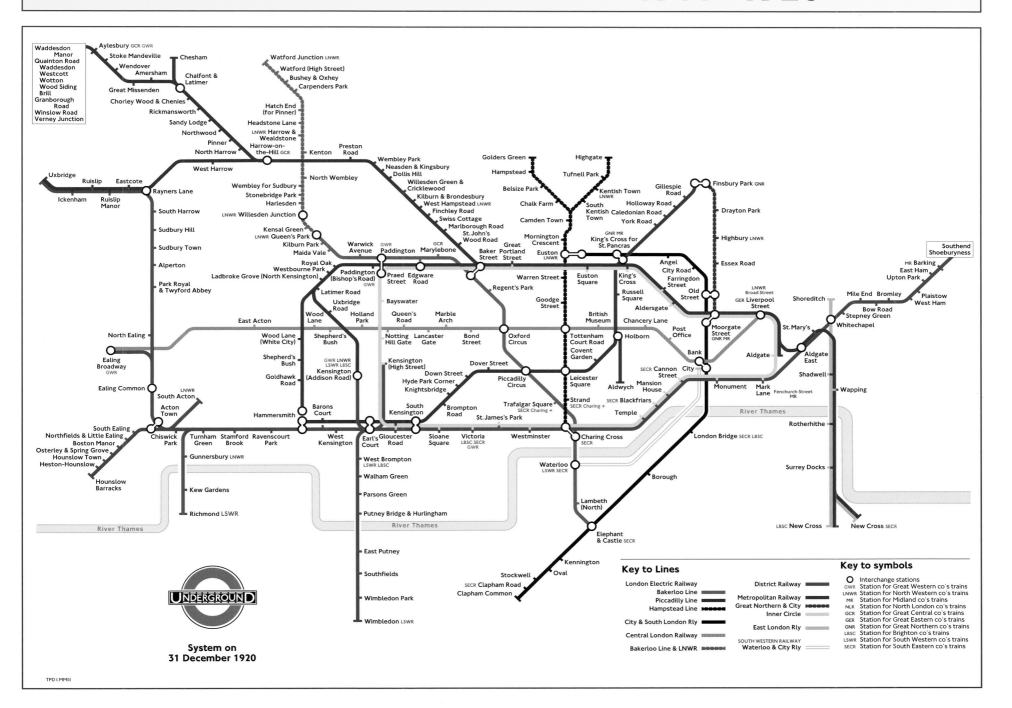

Waddesdon Manor
Quainton Road
Waddesdon
Westcott
Wotton
Wood Siding
Brill
Granborough Road
Winslow Road
Verney Junction

Aylesbury GCR GWR
Stoke Mandeville
Wendover
Amersham
Great Missenden
Chorley Wood & Chenies
Rickmansworth
Sandy Lodge
Northwood
Pinner
North Harrow
West Harrow
Chesham
Chalfont & Latimer
Hatch End (for Pinner)
Headstone Lane
LNWR Harrow & Wealdstone
Harrow-on-the-Hill GCR
Kenton
Preston Road

Watford Junction LNWR
Watford (High Street)
Bushey & Oxhey
Carpenders Park

Uxbridge
Ruislip
Eastcote
Ickenham
Ruislip Manor
Rayners Lane
South Harrow
Sudbury Hill
Sudbury Town
Alperton
Park Royal & Twyford Abbey
North Ealing

Wembley for Sudbury
Stonebridge Park
Harlesden
LNWR Willesden Junction
Kensal Green
LNWR Queen's Park
Kilburn Park
Maida Vale
Royal Oak
Westbourne Park
Ladbroke Grove (North Kensington)

Wembley Park
Neasden & Kingsbury
Dollis Hill
Willesden Green & Cricklewood
Kilburn & Brondesbury
West Hampstead LNWR
Finchley Road
Swiss Cottage
Marlborough Road
St. John's Wood Road
Great Portland Street

Golders Green
Hampstead
Belsize Park
Chalk Farm
Camden Town
South Kentish Town
Kentish Town LNWR
Holloway Road
Caledonian Road
York Road

Highgate
Tufnell Park

Finsbury Park GNR
Gillespie Road
Drayton Park
Highbury LNWR
Essex Road

Southend Shoeburyness

Ealing Broadway GWR
Ealing Common
LNWR South Acton
Acton Town
South Ealing
Northfields & Little Ealing
Boston Manor
Osterley & Spring Grove
Hounslow Town
Heston-Hounslow
Hounslow Barracks

East Acton
Wood Lane (White City)
Shepherd's Bush
Goldhawk Road
GWR LNWR LSWR LBSC
Kensington (Addison Road)
Hammersmith
Barons Court
Chiswick Park
Turnham Green
Stamford Brook
Ravenscourt Park
Gunnersbury LNWR
Kew Gardens
Richmond LSWR

Wood Lane
Latimer Road
Uxbridge Road
Holland Park
Shepherd's Bush

Warwick Avenue
GWR Paddington
Paddington (Bishop's Road) GWR
Praed Street
Edgware Road
Bayswater
Queen's Road
Notting Hill Gate
Kensington (High Street)
Down Street
Hyde Park Corner
Knightsbridge
South Kensington
West Kensington
Earl's Court
Gloucester Road
Sloane Square
West Brompton LSWR LBSC
Walham Green
Parsons Green
Putney Bridge & Hurlingham
East Putney
Southfields
Wimbledon Park
Wimbledon LSWR

GCR Marylebone
Baker Street
Warren Street
Regent's Park
Marble Arch
Lancaster Gate
Bond Street
Oxford Circus
Dover Street
Piccadilly Circus
Brompton Road
Victoria LBSC SECR GWR

Mornington Crescent
Euston LNWR
Euston Square
Goodge Street
British Museum
Tottenham Court Road
Covent Garden
Leicester Square
Trafalgar Square SECR Charing +
Strand SECR Charing +
St. James's Park
Westminster

GNR MR King's Cross for St. Pancras
King's Cross
Russell Square
Chancery Lane
Holborn
King's Cross
Post Office
Aldersgate
Angel
City Road
Farringdon Street
Old Street

Bank
Mansion House
SECR Cannon Street
City
Monument
SECR Blackfriars
Temple
Charing Cross SECR

Moorgate Street GNR MR
Aldgate
Mark Lane
Fenchurch Street MR
LNWR Broad Street
GER Liverpool Street
St. Mary's
Aldgate East
Shadwell

Shoreditch
Whitechapel
Mile End Bromley
Bow Road
Stepney Green
MR Barking
East Ham
Upton Park
Plaistow
West Ham
Wapping
Rotherhithe
Surrey Docks
River Thames

London Bridge SECR LBSC
Borough
Lambeth (North)
Waterloo LSWR SECR
Kennington
Oval
Stockwell
SECR Clapham Road
Clapham Common
Elephant & Castle SECR
LBSC New Cross
New Cross SECR

UNDERGROUND

**System on
31 December 1920**

TPD I.MMIII

1921–1930

Principal developments of the decade

Centre right The entrance to Hendon Central station as first built in open countryside in November 1923.

Far right The same station entrance once it had been enveloped by shops and flats at the end of the same decade.

Right The original Piccadilly Circus booking hall connected to the platforms by lifts was replaced, from 1928, by the present circular concourse and eleven escalators. Many of the original features can still be seen, such as the world clock and panelled ceiling. Others, sadly missing, are the fluted ceiling lamp-shades either side of the columns which were destroyed when fluorescent lighting was installed in the 1950s, but not re-instated when the concourse was restored.

Below Detail from a poster of the 1920s showing a typical tube station, with a train of Standard Stock.

Hampstead & Highgate Line and City & South London Railway

1923 Golders Green to Hendon opened on 19 November.

1924 Moorgate to Euston re-opened after reconstruction. Through running inaugurated via Camden Town to join the Hampstead & Highgate Line on 20 April.

1924 Hendon to Edgware opened from 18 August.

1924 Bank to Clapham Common re-opened with enlarged tunnels to take Standard Tube Stock on 1 December.

1926 Clapham Common to Morden, and through running via Kennington to Hampstead & Highgate Line, from 13 September.

Waterloo & City Railway [LSWR]

1923 Became part of the Southern Railway on 1 January.

Metropolitan Railway

1925 Branch from north of Sandy Lodge to Watford, with one intermediate station at Croxley Green, opened with a joint service with the LNER on 2 November.

Bakerloo and Piccadilly Lines

1928 The rebuilt Piccadilly Circus station, with its circular concourse, opened on 10 December.

Piccadilly Line

1930 Civil engineering commenced on extensions to both ends of the line, from Finsbury Park towards Arnos Grove in the north and from Hammersmith towards Acton Town in the west.

HENDON, CENTRAL STATION

Opening dates of stations, name changes and closures

Stations opened or first served by Underground trains

26.06.1923	Northwick Park & Kenton	MetR
5.11.1923	North Acton	CLR
5.11.1923	West Acton	CLR
19.11.1923	Brent	CCE&HR
19.11.1923	Hendon Central	CCE&HR
10.12.1923	Hillingdon	Met MDR
23.04.1924	Wembley Park Exhibition	MetR
18.08.1924	Colindale	CCE&HR
18.08.1924	Edgware	CCE&HR
27.10.1924	Burnt Oak	CCE&HR
2.11.1925	Croxley Green	MetR-LNER JOINT
2.11.1925	Watford	MetR-LNER JOINT
13.09.1926	Balham	C&SLR
13.09.1926	Clapham South	C&SLR
13.09.1926	Colliers Wood	C&SLR
13.09.1926	Morden	C&SLR
13.09.1926	South Wimbledon	C&SLR
13.09.1926	Tooting Broadway	C&SLR
13.09.1926	Trinity Road (Tooting Bec)	C&SLR
13.09.1926	Waterloo	CCE&HR

Station names changed

	from	to
26.01.1922	Farringdon Street	Farringdon & High Holborn
12.03.1922	Amersham	Amersham & Chesham Bois
20.07.1922	Essex Road	Canonbury & Essex Road
20.07.1922	Highbury	Highbury & Islington
1.10.1922	Waddesdon Manor	Waddesdon
1.10.1922	Waddesdon [O&AT]	Waddesdon Road
1923	Bayswater	Bayswater (Queen's Road) & Westbourne Grove
1923	Great Portland Street	Great Portland Street & Regent's Park
1923	Aldersgate	Aldersgate & Barbican
26.01.1923	St.Mary's	St.Mary's (Whitechapel Road)
9.07.1923	New Cross [LBSC]	New Cross Gate
18.10.1923	Sandy Lodge	Moor Park & Sandy Lodge
11.02.1924	West Ham	West Ham (Manor Road)
20.04.1924	Moorgate Street [MetRI]	Moorgate
1925	King's Cross [MetR]	King's Cross & St.Pancras
1.04.1925	St.John's Wood Road	St.John's Wood
1.12.1925	Hounslow Town	Hounslow East
1.12.1925	Heston Hounslow	Hounslow Central
1.12.1925	Hounslow Barracks	Hounslow West
13.09.1926	Clapham Road	Clapham North
1927	King's Cross [GNP&BR]	King's Cross for St.Pancras
1927	Lambeth (North)	Lambeth North
1.03.1927	*Mill Hill Barracks [LNER]*	*Mill Hill (East) for Mill Hill Barracks [LNER]*
1928	Burnt Oak	Burnt Oak (Watling)

Stations last served by Underground trains

8.08.1922	City Road	C&SLR
5.06.1924	South Kentish Town	CCE&HR

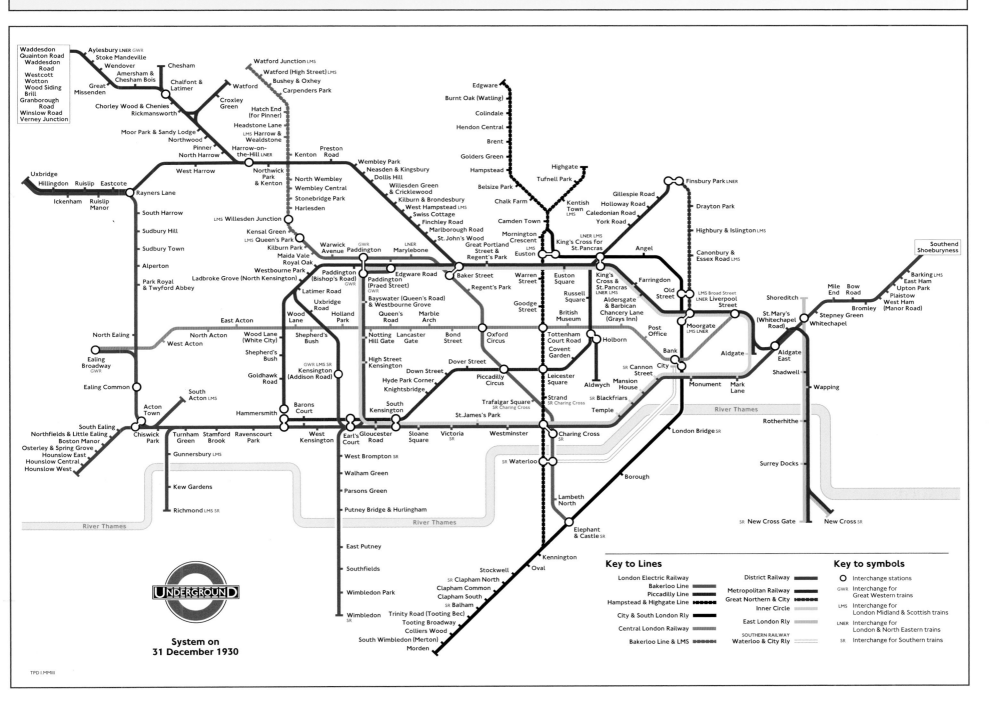

**System on
31 December 1930**

Key to Lines

London Electric Railway		District Railway
Bakerloo Line		Metropolitan Railway
Piccadilly Line		Great Northern & City
Hampstead & Highgate Line		Inner Circle
City & South London Rly		East London Rly
Central London Railway		SOUTHERN RAILWAY
Bakerloo Line & LMS		Waterloo & City Rly

Key to symbols

O   Interchange stations
GWR   Interchange for Great Western trains
LMS   Interchange for London Midland & Scottish trains
LNER   Interchange for London & North Eastern trains
SR   Interchange for Southern trains

TPD I.MMIII

Principal developments of the decade

Above right One era closes as another opens. The Metropolitan Line's tranquil Granborough Road station, which lost its passenger service in 1934, contrasts with a 'streamlined' tube train of 1935.

Below Osterley station, new in 1934, was one of a number designed in the 1920s and '30s for the Underground by the architect Charles Holden.

Bakerloo Line

1933 Became the Bakerloo Line of the London Passenger Transport Board on 1 July.

1939 Bakerloo trains run to Stanmore, through new tunnels from Baker Street to Finchley Road and over former Metropolitan tracks, from 20 November.

Central London Railway

1933 Became the Central London Line of the London Passenger Transport Board on 1 July.

1937 Was re-named the Central Line from August 1937.

C&SLR and Hampstead & Highgate Line

1933 Both were combined as the Morden–Edgware Line of the London Passenger Transport Board on 1 July.

1937 In preparation for the opening of the extensions to Edgware (via Mill Hill), High Barnet and Alexandra Palace the line was renamed Northern Line, in August.

1939 Electric traction to East Finchley from 3 July.

1940 Electric traction to High Barnet from 14 April.

Great Northern & City Railway

1933 Became the Northern City Line of the London Passenger Transport Board on 1 July.

1939 Original main line size rolling stock replaced by Tube stock on 15 May, in preparation for the line's amalgamation with the Northern Line.

Metropolitan Railway

1932 Branch to Stanmore opened on 10 December.

1933 Became the Metropolitan Line of the London Passenger Transport Board on 1 July.

1939 Haulage of GWR Windsor trains by Metropolitan electric locomotives discontinued between Paddington and Aldgate on 16 September.

1939 Pullman cars withdrawn from trains between Aylesbury and Chesham to Baker Street and Aldgate on 7 October.

1940 First Class accommodation withdrawn from Metropolitan Line trains from 1 February.

Metropolitan District Railway

1932 Through working over LMS line to Upminster began on 12 September.

1933 Became the District Line of the London Passenger Transport Board on 1 July.

1933 District Line service between Ealing and Uxbridge transferred to Piccadilly Line operation from 24 October

Piccadilly Tube

1932 Tube trains start working over District Line to South Harrow via Hammersmith and Acton Town from 4 June.

1932 Finsbury Park to Arnos Grove from 19 September.

1933 Arnos Grove to Enfield West, with through services to Hounslow West, from 13 March.

1933 Became the Piccadilly Line of the London Passenger Transport Board on 1 July.

1933 Enfield West to Cockfosters from 31 July.

1933 Through service to Uxbridge from 23 October.

Waterloo & City Railway

1940 Re-signalled and new Southern Railway designed rolling stock brought into service on 28 October.

PRINCIPAL AMALGAMATIONS

1933 The newly incorporated London Passenger Transport Board acquired the undertakings of the City & South London Railway, the Central London Railway, the London Electric Railway, the Metropolitan Railway and the Metropolitan District Railway, on 1 July.

Station names changed

	from	to
1931	King's Cross & St.Pancras *first site*	King's Cross St.Pancras
1932	Putney Bridge & Hurlingham	Putney Bridge
1.01.1932	Neasden & Kingsbury	Neasden
18.07.1932	Gale Street	Becontree
12.09.1932	*Northolt Junction [GWR]*	*South Ruislip Northolt Junction [GWR]*
31.10.1932	Gillespie Road	Arsenal (Highbury Hill)
1933	Canons Park (Edgware)	Canons Park
1933	Great Portland Street & Regent's Park	Great Portland Street
1933	Bayswater (Queen's Road) & Westbourne Grove	Bayswater
1933	King's Cross for St.Pancras MORDEN–EDGWARE/PICCADILLY	King's Cross St.Pancras
22.05.1933	Holborn	Holborn (Kingsway)
10.09.1933	Paddington (Bishop's Road)	Paddington
18.09.1933	Dover Street	Green Park
1934	Amersham & Chesham Bois	Amersham
1934	Chorley Wood & Chenies	Chorley Wood
20.04.1934	Hillingdon	Hillingdon (Swakeleys)
3.05.1934	Enfield West	Enfield West (Oakwood)
25.06.1935	Chancery Lane	Chancery Lane (Gray's Inn)
1.03.1936	Park Royal	Park Royal (Hanger Hill)
21.04.1936	Farringdon & High Holborn	Farringdon
1.02.1937	Post Office	St.Paul's
15.03.1937	Northwick Park & Kenton	Northwick Park
5.07.1937	*George Lane [LNER]*	*South Woodford (George Lane) [LNER]*
1938	Ladbroke Grove (North Kensington)	Ladbroke Grove
1938	Willesden Green & Cricklewood	Willesden Green
11.06.1939	Highgate	Archway (Highgate)
1.06.1939	St.John's Wood MET	Lord's
1.04.1940	*Finchley (Church End)*	*Finchley Central [LNER]*
28.10.1940	*City [Waterloo & City]*	*Bank [Waterloo & City]*

Stations last served by Underground trains

5.07.1931	Park Royal & Twyford Abbey LER - PICCADILLY
21.11.1931	Preston Road London-bound side MetR *first site*
2.01.1932	Preston Road country-bound side MetR *first site*
18.05.1932	Northfields & Little Ealing LER - PICCADILLY *first site*
21.05.1932	Down Street LER - PICCADILLY
17.09.1932	York Road LER - PICCADILLY
24.09.1933	British Museum CENTRAL LONDON LINE
29.07.1934	Brompton Road PICCADILLY LINE
30.11.1935	Brill § METROPOLITAN LINE
30.11.1935	Waddesdon Road METROPOLITAN LINE
30.11.1935	Westcott § METROPOLITAN LINE
30.11.1935	Wood Siding § METROPOLITAN LINE
30.11.1935	Wotton § METROPOLITAN LINE
4.07.1936	Granborough Road [Met&GCJt] METROPOLITAN LINE
4.07.1936	Winslow Road [Met&GCJt] METROPOLITAN LINE
4.07.1936	Verney Junction [Met&GCJt] MET LINE *still served by LMS*
5.07.1936	Quainton Road [Met&GCJt] MET LINE *still served by LNER*
5.07.1936	Waddesdon [Met&GCJt] MET LINE *still served by LNER*
30.04.1938	St.Mary's DISTRICT/METROPOLITAN LINES
30.10.1938	Aldgate East DISTRICT/METROPOLITAN LINES *first site*
3.12.1938	Uxbridge METROPOLITAN/PICCADILLY LINES *first site*
19.11.1939	Marlborough Road METROPOLITAN LINE
19.11.1939	Lord's METROPOLITAN LINE
17.08.1940	Swiss Cottage METROPOLITAN LINE
21.09.1940	Aldwych PICCADILLY LINE
19.10.1940	Kensington (Addison Road) DISTRICT/METROPOLITAN LINES
19.10.1940	Uxbridge Road METROPOLITAN LINE

Leaflets were produced at an ever increasing rate advertising the new extensions as they were opened.

Opening dates of stations, name changes and closures

Stations opened or first served by Underground trains

6.07.1931	Park Royal LER - PICCADILLY *present site*	
22.11.1931	Preston Road London-bound side MetR *present site*	
3.01.1932	Preston Road country-bound side MetR *present site*	
19.05.1932	Northfields MDR *present site*	
12.09.1932	Barking MDR *re-served*	
12.09.1932	Becontree MDR	
2.09.1932	Dagenham MDR *re-served*	
12.09.1932	Heathway MDR	
12.09.1932	Hornchurch MDR *re-served*	
12.09.1932	Upminster MDR *re-served*	
12.09.1932	Upney MDR	
19.09.1932	Arnos Grove LER - PICCADILLY	
19.09.1932	Bounds Green LER - PICCADILLY	
19.09.1932	Manor House LER - PICCADILLY	
19.09.1932	Turnpike Lane LER - PICCADILLY	
19.09.1932	Wood Green LER - PICCADILLY	
10.12.1932	Canons Park (Edgware) MetR	
10.12.1932	Kingsbury MetR	
10.12.1932	Stanmore MetR	
1.03.1933	West Finchley [LNER]	
13.03.1933	Enfield West LER - PICCADILLY	
13.03.1933	Southgate LER - PICCADILLY	
3.07.1933	South Kenton MetR	
31.07.1933	Cockfosters LER - PICCADILLY	
25.09.1933	Holborn (Kingsway) CENTRAL LONDON LINE	
13.11.1933	Northwood Hills METROPOLITAN LINE	
25.03.1934	Osterley DISTRICT/PICCADILLY LINES *present site*	
16.12.1934	Queensbury METROPOLITAN LINE	
17.12.1934	Upminster Bridge DISTRICT LINE	
13.05.1935	Elm Park DISTRICT LINE	
31.10.1938	Aldgate East DISTRICT/METROPOLITAN LINES *present site*	
4.12.1938	Uxbridge METROPOLITAN/PICCADILLY LINES *present site*	
3.07.1939	East Finchley NORTHERN LINE *	
20.11.1939	St.John's Wood BAKERLOO LINE	
20.11.1939	Swiss Cottage BAKERLOO LINE	
14.04.1940	High Barnet NORTHERN LINE *	
14.04.1940	Finchley Central NORTHERN LINE *	
14.04.1940	High Barnet NORTHERN LINE *	
14.04.1940	Totteridge & Whetstone NORTHERN LINE *	
14.04.1940	West Finchley NORTHERN LINE *	
14.04.1940	Woodside Park NORTHERN LINE *	
28.04.1940	*Loughton [LNER] present site*	

§ Stations remained the property of the Oxford & Aylesbury Tramroad Company controlled by the Trustees of the late Earl Temple's Estate.

* Stations originally opened by GNR 1.04.1872

**System on
31 December 1940**

LONDON TRANSPORT

TPD I.MMIII

Key to Lines

Bakerloo

Central
under construction

Circle

District

East London

Metropolitan

Northern
under construction

Northern City section

Piccadilly

SOUTHERN RAILWAY
Waterloo & City

Key to symbols

O Interchange stations

GWR Interchange for
Great Western trains

LMS Interchange for
London Midland & Scottish trains

LNER Interchange for
London & North Eastern trains

SR Interchange for Southern trains

Principal developments of the decade

Maps displayed in the advertisement panels of compartment stock, tracing the Metropolitan Line's country network, employed two distinct styles: that showing the steam section to Aylesbury was drawn in a geographic style reflecting the leisurely tone associated with the mode of travel, while that covering the electrified section was drawn to the prevailing diagram standards.

Northern Line

1941 The new Highgate station opened on 19 January with interchange for the Alexandra Palace branch, already equipped for electric operation to become part of the Northern Line.

1941 Electric trains commenced running over Finchley Central to Edgware branch, but only as far as Mill Hill East, on 18 May.

Central Line

1946 First post-war extension from Liverpool Street to Stratford opened on 4 December.

1947 Eastern extension from Stratford to Leyton and Leytonstone opened on 5 May.

1947 Western extension from North Acton to Greenford opened on 30 June.

1947 Both branches opened from Leytonstone: one through tube tunnels to Newbury Park; the other over LNER tracks to Woodford, on 14 December.

1948 Newbury Park to Hainault electric service replaced British Railways steam trains from 31 May.

1948 Eastern Region steam trains replaced on the extension from Woodford to Loughton and the branch from Loughton to Hainault via Roding Valley from 21 November. On same day, electric services to West Ruislip replaced local Western Region steam trains.

1949 Electric trains replaced Eastern Region steam from Loughton to Epping on 25 September.

Piccadilly Line

1940 Aldwych branch and station closed for the duration of the war, on 21 October, re-opening in 1946 on 1 July.

Waterloo & City Railway

1948 Became part of British Railways Southern Region on 1 January.

PRINCIPAL AMALGAMATIONS

1948 Authority and assets of the London Passenger Transport Board passed to the London Transport Executive of the state-owned British Transport Commission on 1 January.

SPIT-AND-POLISH

In peace-time, LONDON TRANSPORT used hundreds of tons of soap and millions of gallons of water every week for cleaning; thousands of brooms and brushes were worn out.

To-day, of course, shortage of staff and materials has reduced these figures, but still we try to present a clean, shining face to our passengers every morning. Habits die hard, and the traditional spit-and-polish of LONDON TRANSPORT has survived even the repressive influence of war-time stringency.

Acton Town in August 1948, with a Piccadilly Line train of Standard Stock ready to leave for Hounslow, while a District Line train headed by an E Class motor car, with hand operated doors and dating from 1910, stands at the London bound platform.

The trains introduced by the Metropolitan Railway in the 1920s to work the Circle Line service lasted until the very end of this decade, the last of the class being withdrawn on 31 December 1950.

Opening dates of stations, name changes and closures

Stations opened or first served by Underground trains

19.01.1941	Highgate	*present site* *
14.03.1941	King's Cross St.Pancras	METROPOLITAN LINE *present site*
18.05.1941	Mill Hill East *	*opened by GNR 22.08.1867*
5.04.1943	Quainton Road	METROPOLITAN LINE *station re-served*
4.12.1946	Bethnal Green ¶	
4.12.1946	Mile End ¶	
4.12.1946	Stratford [LNER] ¶	*opened by ECR 22.08.1856*
20.12.1946	Kensington (Olympia)	DISTRICT LINE *exhibitions only*
5.05.1947	Leyton ¶	*opened by ECR 22.08 1856*
5.05.1947	Leytonstone ¶	*opened by ECR 22.08 1856*
30.06.1947	Greenford ¶	*opened by GWR 1.10.1904*
30.06.1947	Hanger Lane ¶	*opened by GWR 1.05.1904*
30.06.1947	Perivale ¶	*opened by GWR 1.05.1904*
23.11.1947	White City ¶	
14.12.1947	Gants Hill ¶	
14.12.1947	Newbury Park ¶	
14.12.1947	Redbridge ¶	
14.12.1947	South Woodford (George Lane) ¶	*opened by ECR 22.08 1856*
14.12.1947	Snaresbrook ¶	*opened by ECR 22.08 1856*
14.12.1947	Wanstead ¶	
14.12.1947	Woodford ¶	*opened by ECR 22.08 1856*
31.05.1948	Barkingside ¶	*opened by GER 1.05.1903*
31.05.1948	Fairlop ¶	*opened by GER 1.05.1903*
31.05.1948	Hainault ¶	*opened by GER 1.05.1903*
21.11.1948	Buckhurst Hill ¶	*opened by ECR 22.08 1856*
21.11.1948	Chigwell ¶	*opened by GER 1.05.1903*
21.11.1948	Grange Hill ¶	*opened by GER 1.05.1903*
21.11.1948	Loughton ¶	*opened by ECR 22.08 1856*
21.11.1948	Northolt ¶	*opened by GWR 1.05.1907*
21.11.1948	Roding Valley ¶	*opened by GER 1.05.1903*
21.11.1948	Ruislip Gardens ¶	*opened by GW&GCJt 9.07.1934*
21.11.1948	South Ruislip	*opened by GW&GCJt 1.05.1908*
21.11.1948	West Ruislip ¶	*opened by GW&GCJt 1.02.1906*
25.09.1949	Blake Hall ¶	*opened by ECR 1.04.1865*
25.09.1949	Debden ¶	*opened by ECR 1.04.1865*
25.09.1949	Epping ¶	*opened by ECR 1.04.1865*
25.09.1949	North Weald ¶	*opened by ECR 1.04.1865*
25.09.1949	Ongar ¶	*opened by ECR 1.04.1865*
25.09.1949	Theydon Bois ¶	*opened by ECR 1.04.1865*

* Northern Line stations   ¶ Central Line stations

Station names changed

Date	from	to
19.01.1941	Archway (Highgate)	Highgate (Archway)
1.09.1946	Bayswater (Queen's Road)	Bayswater (Queensway)
1.09.1946	Enfield West (Oakwood)	Oakwood
1.09.1946	Mark Lane	Tower Hill
1.09.1946	Queen's Road	Queensway
1947	Park Royal (Hanger Hill)	Park Royal
30.06.1947	*South Ruislip & Northolt Junction*	*South Ruislip [GWR]*
30.06.1947	*Ruislip & Ickenham*	*West Ruislip (for Ickenham) [GWR]*
23.11.1947	Wood Lane (White City)	White City
12.1947	Highgate (Archway)	Archway
5.07.1948	Wembley for Sudbury	Wembley Central
11.07.1948	Canonbury & Essex Road	Essex Road
11.07.1947	Paddington (Praed Street)	Paddington
1.05.1949	Dagenham	Dagenham East
1.05.1949	Heathway	Dagenham Heathway
23.05.1949	Croxley Green	Croxley
1950	South Woodford (George Lane)	South Woodford
25.09.1950	Aylesbury [BR(E)]	Aylesbury Town [BR(E)]
25.09.1950	Moor Park & Sandy Lodge	Moor Park
25.09.1950	Kilburn & Brondesbury	Kilburn
1.10.1950	Trinity Road (Tooting Bec)	Tooting Bec

Stations last served by Underground trains

13.03.1941	King's Cross	METROPOLITAN LINE *first site*
22.11.1947	Wood Lane	CENTRAL LINE
29.05.1948	Quainton Road	METROPOLITAN LINE *still open for BR(E)*

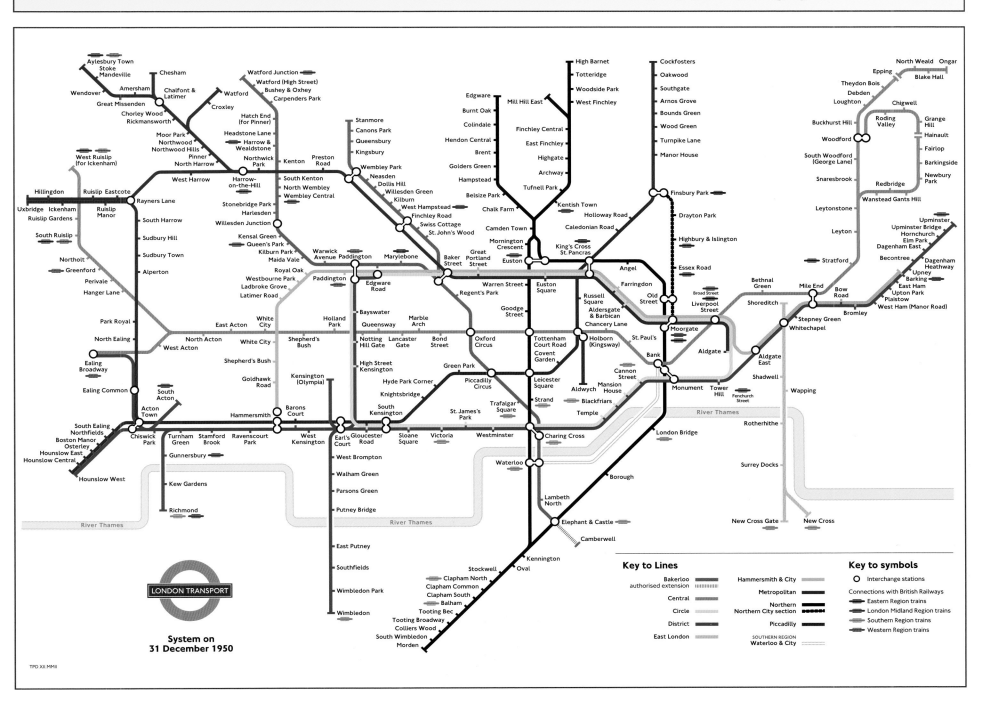

**System on
31 December 1950**

TPD XII.MMII

Key to Lines

Bakerloo		Hammersmith & City	
authorised extension		Metropolitan	
Central		Northern	
Circle		Northern City section	
District		Piccadilly	
East London		SOUTHERN REGION Waterloo & City	

Key to symbols

○ Interchange stations

Connections with British Railways

Eastern Region trains
London Midland Region trains
Southern Region trains
Western Region trains

Principal developments of the decade

District Line

1953 First train of unpainted aluminium stock enters service on 19 January.

Northern Line

1954 Official abandonment, on 9 February, of all unfinished portions of the pre-war new works scheme. These were: extension beyond Edgware to Bushey Heath; electrification of steam worked line beyond Mill Hill East to Edgware; connection between Finsbury Park and Highgate; Alexandra Palace branch from Highgate.

Central Line

1957 Tube stock replaced the steam trains provided by British Railways Eastern Region on the single line Epping – Ongar section, on 18 November. This completed the 82.48km (51¼ mile) programme of Central Line extensions and electrictrification of former main line routes.

Metropolitan Line

1960 The electrified rails reached out to Amersham and Chesham on 12 September 1960.

Opening dates of stations, name changes and closures

Stations opened or first served by Underground trains
17.11.1952 Carpenders Park BAKERLOO LINE *present site*

Station names changed

	from	*to*
2.03.1952	Walham Green	Fulham Broadway
1956	Hatch End (for Pinner)	Hatch End

Stations last served by Underground trains
16.11.1952 Carpenders Park BAKERLOO LINE *first site*
28.02.1959 South Acton DISTRICT LINE *remained open for BR(M)*
21.10.1959 White City METROPOLITAN LINE

One of the Underground's first unpainted aluminium cars of R Stock for the District Line, which entered service in 1953.

Epping was the eastern terminal point of the electrified Central Line from 1950 – the electrification of the single line extension to Ongar followed in November 1957. Until conversion, steam trains continued to be provided by British Railways Eastern Region. A shuttle train is seen here at Epping in the early 1950s, waiting for the Central Line tube to arrive from London, before returning to Ongar.

A system of directions to central London main line terminal stations, using colour coded lights, guided passengers through interchanges between lines.

But the main problem was that the directional colours to be followed often differed from those of the lines to be used, which led to this fundamentally useful idea being abandoned.

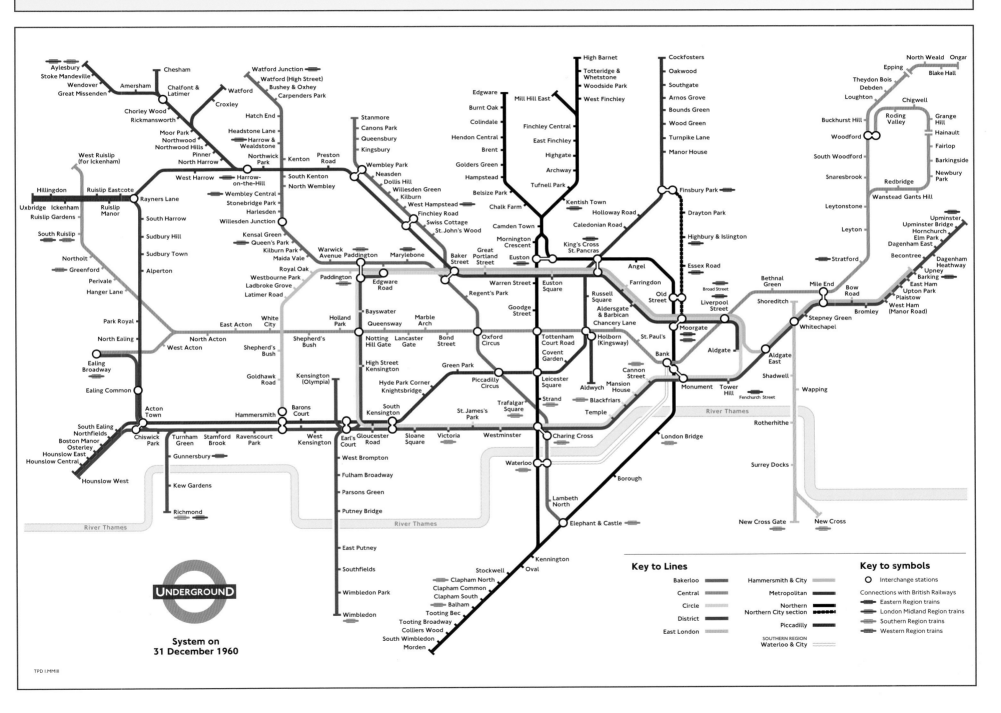

**System on
31 December 1960**

Key to Lines

Bakerloo	Hammersmith & City
Central	Metropolitan
Circle	Northern
District	Northern City section
East London	Piccadilly

SOUTHERN REGION
Waterloo & City

Key to symbols

○ Interchange stations

Connections with British Railways
— Eastern Region trains
— London Midland Region trains
— Southern Region trains
— Western Region trains

TPD.I.MMIII

Principal developments of the decade

Central Line

1963 The Woodford – Hainault section was experimentally converted for signals from the track to send messages for the newly designed motor cars of 1960 Stock to be driven automatically. Apart from some tests of equipment on the District Line, this was the first use of automatic train operation on London's Underground.

Metropolitan Line

1961 Full through electric service introduced between Baker Street and Amersham and on the Chesham branch. Withdrawal of Metropolitan Line trains north of Amersham – the manning of stations and operation of the diesel train service beyond was transferred completely to British Railways London Midland Region – from 9 September.

Northern Line – Northern City section

1964 Drayton Park becomes the northern terminus, as a consequence of the Finsbury Park station tunnels being adapted to form part of the Victoria Line, on 5 October.

Victoria Line

1962 The Government sanctions the building of the Victoria Line – between Victoria and Walthamstow (Hoe Street) – a distance of 16.1km (10½ miles).

1968 The initial section of London's first new Underground line for 60 years opened between Walthamstow Central and Highbury & Islington on 1 September. Its automatic operation and trains were evolved from the experimental prototypes developed on the Woodford – Hainault section of the Central Line.

1968 Services commenced on the second section between Highbury & Islington and Warren Street on 1 December.

1969 The line through to Victoria was opened by Queen Elizabeth II on 7 March.

Opening dates of stations, name changes and closures

Stations opened or first served by Underground trains

5.02.1967	Tower Hill	DISTRICT LINE *present site*
1.09.1968	Blackhorse Road	VICTORIA LINE
1.09.1968	Finsbury Park	VICTORIA LINE
1.09.1968	Highbury & Islington	VICTORIA LINE
1.09.1968	Seven Sisters	VICTORIA LINE
1.09.1968	Tottenham Hale	VICTORIA LINE
1.09.1968	Walthamstow Central	VICTORIA LINE
1.12.1968	Euston	VICTORIA LINE
1.12.1968	King's Cross St.Pancras	VICTORIA LINE
1.12.1968	Warren Street	VICTORIA LINE
7.03.1969	Green Park	VICTORIA LINE
7.03.1969	Oxford Circus	VICTORIA LINE
7.03.1969	Victoria	VICTORIA LINE

Station names changed

	from	to
1964	Chorley Wood	Chorleywood
18.05.1967	Bromley	Bromley-by-Bow
6.05.1968	*Hoe Street Walthamstow*	*Walthamstow Central*
1.12.1968	Aldersgate & Barbican	Barbican
1.01.1969	West Ham (Manor Road)	West Ham

Stations last served by Underground trains

10.09.1961	Great Missenden	METROPOLITAN LINE	*transferred to BR*
10.09.1961	Wendover	METROPOLITAN LINE	*transferred to BR*
10.09.1961	Stoke Mandeville	METROPOLITAN LINE	*transferred to BR*
10.09.1961	Aylesbury Town [BR]	METROPOLITAN LINE	*remained open for BR*
4.02.1967	Tower Hill	DISTRICT LINE	*first site*

Part of the fleet of automatic trains pose outside their Northumberland Park depot prior to the opening of the Victoria Line in 1968.

A Metropolitan Line steam train runs for the last time on the Chalfont & Latimer to Chesham branch. In 1936 haulage of LT passenger trains was devolved to LNER (and later British Railways) engines and crews. The carriages remained LT property and those used on the Chesham branch held the distinction of being the oldest in the fleet, dating from 1898.

VICTORIA LINE
Exhibition at the Design Centre
August 21 – September 28, 1968
SOUVENIR TICKET

Peggy Healey, of London Transport's Publicity Office, tries out the experimental automatic gates at Hammersmith District and Piccadilly lines ticket office.

SOUTH KENSINGTON (D) 2   1/3
To any one of L.T. stations shown on fares list at SINGLE FARE of

For automatic gates
INSERT THIS WAY →

Issued subject to LONDON TRANSPORT Bye-laws, Regulations and Conditions. Valid day of issue only.

55808

LONDON TRANSPORT   1
LAST DAY OF STEAM SHUTTLE OPERATION
11th SEPTEMBER, 1960
CHALFONT & LATIMER
to
CHESHAM
2nd Cl.   Fare 10d
For conditions see over

0084

41272

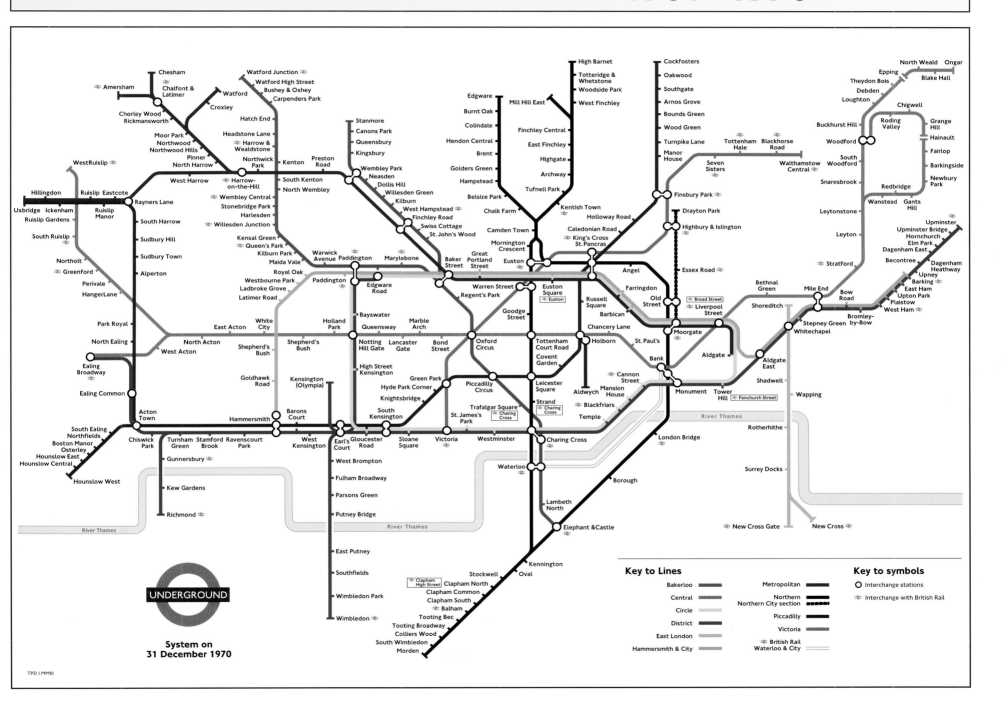

Key to Lines

Bakerloo	Metropolitan
Central	Northern
Circle	Northern City section
District	Piccadilly
East London	Victoria
Hammersmith & City	British Rail
	Waterloo & City

Key to symbols

○ Interchange stations

≡ Interchange with British Rail

UNDERGROUND

System on
31 December 1970

TPD I.MMIII

Principal developments of the decade

Decimalisation

1971 All ticket machines were altered and pre-printed tickets re-stocked for the change of currency.

Right Steam on the Underground peeped into the decade of the 1970s. Kept for hauling maintenance trains, usually when the electric system was closed for the night, they bowed out in 1971 with a ceremony announced in this strikingly simple poster.

Far right Most of the Jubilee Line ran over the former Bakerloo branch from Baker Street to Stanmore.

Right Work proceeded on the airport extension during the 1970s, resulting in re-sited platforms at Hounslow West and completely new stations at Hatton Cross and the terminus, shown here, Heathrow Central.

Metropolitan Line

1971 The Underground's steam locomotives, used for the haulage of engineers' trains, were withdrawn, followed by a commemorative run from Barbican to Neasden depot on 6 June.

Victoria Line

1971 The extension southwards from Victoria to Brixton opened, together with intermediate stations at Vauxhall and Stockwell, on 23 July.

1972 Pimlico Station, for the Tate Gallery, opened on 14 September.

Piccadilly Line

1971 Building began on the 5.6km (3½ mile) extension from Hounslow West to Heathrow Airport, with an intermediate station at Hatton Cross, in April 1971.

1975 Hatton Cross opened on 19 July.

1977 London Airport was connected by tube to central London with the opening of Heathrow Central on 16 December.

Jubilee Line

1972 Work commenced on the first stage of tunnelling of what was originally called the Fleet Line, between Baker Street and Charing Cross.

1977 The name was changed to Jubilee Line to mark the Silver Jubilee of the accession to the throne of Queen Elizabeth II in 1952.

1979 The line between Stanmore and Baker Street (formerly part of the Bakerloo Line and originally operated by the Metropolitan Railway) and the new tunnel section to Charing Cross, was opened by HRH The Prince of Wales on 30 April 1979 and to the public the following day.

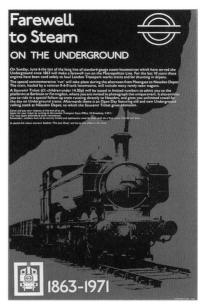

Northern Line – Northern City section

1975 Tube rolling stock ran for the last time on 3 October, in preparation for the line's transfer to British Rail and its re-conversion to take main line size trains.

Opening dates of stations, name changes and closures

Stations opened or first served by Underground trains

23.07.1971	Brixton	VICTORIA LINE	
23.07.1971	Vauxhall	VICTORIA LINE	
23.07.1971	Stockwell	VICTORIA LINE	
14.09.1972	Pimlico	VICTORIA LINE	
19.07.1975	Hatton Cross	PICCADILLY LINE	
16.12.1977	Heathrow Central	PICCADILLY LINE	
1.05.1979	Baker Street	JUBILEE LINE	
1.05.1979	Bond Street	JUBILEE LINE	
1.05.1979	Charing Cross	JUBILEE LINE	
1.05.1979	Charing Cross	NORTHERN LINE	*re-built from Strand*
1.05.1979	Green Park	JUBILEE LINE	

Station names changed

Date	from	to
6.05.1974	Bushey & Oxhey	Bushey
4.08.1974	Charing Cross	Charing Cross Embankment
20.07.1974	Brent	Brent Cross
12.09.1976	Charing Cross Embankment	Embankment
1.05.1979	Trafalgar Square BAKERLOO LINE	Charing Cross for Trafalgar Square
1.05.1979	Strand NORTHERN LINE	Charing Cross

Stations last served by Underground trains

16.06.1973	Strand	NORTHERN LINE	
6.09.1975	Moorgate	NORTHERN CITY	*transferred to BR*
3.10.1975	Essex Road	NORTHERN CITY	*transferred to BR*
4.10.1975	Drayton Park	NORTHERN CITY	*transferred to BR*
4.10.1975	Highbury & Islington	NORTHERN CITY	*transferred to BR*
4.10.1975	Old Street	NORTHERN CITY	*transferred to BR*

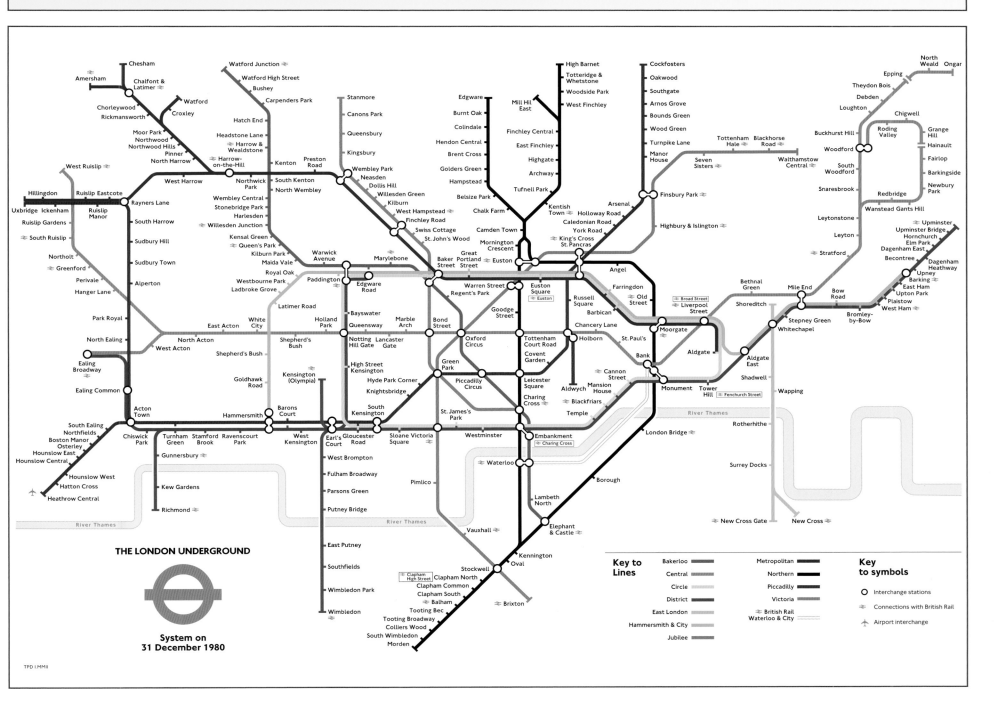

THE LONDON UNDERGROUND

**System on
31 December 1980**

TPD I.MMII

Key to Lines
- Bakerloo
- Central
- Circle
- District
- East London
- Hammersmith & City
- Jubilee
- Metropolitan
- Northern
- Piccadilly
- Victoria
- British Rail Waterloo & City

Key to symbols
- ◯ Interchange stations
- ⇌ Connections with British Rail
- ✈ Airport interchange

Exterior and interior views of the Jubilee Line 1983 Stock. The fleet of trains was scrapped after only 16 years, when replaced by entirely new stock built for the opening of the extension to Stratford in 1999. The use of single-leaf doors followed those installed on the District Line D78 Stock, but were a cause of congestion on the smaller tube stock. Flat fronts to the driving cars lacked the finesse of traditional bow fronts. On the credit side, the cars had very spacious looking interiors, decorated in yellow and orange. They were also the first Underground trains to be controlled with the aid of computer chips.

Principal developments of the decade

Right 'Art on the Underground' was a new series of posters, evolved in the 1980s.

Centre right A test train on the Docklands Light Railway, shortly before it was opened to the public on 31 August 1987.

Below Zonal fares were introduced on a small scale in 1981 with flat fares within a west-central zone and an east-central zone. This system was enlarged in 1983 to cover the entire London Transport bus and Underground networks within the Greater London area, extending outwards in five concentric circles from a single central zone.

Bakerloo Line

1982 Trains withdrawn between Wembley Park and Watford Junction, leaving British Rail in total charge of providing the service, on 24 September.

1984 Tube trains were re-instated between Stonebridge Park and Harrow & Wealdstone on 4 June.

The new Kew by Tube
The Princess of Wales Conservatory. Nearest station Kew Gardens

Piccadilly Line

1986 A single-line loop from Hatton Cross to the existing Heathrow Central was constructed underground. An intermediate station serving Terminal 4 opened on 12 April.

Staff reductions

1985 Circle and Hammersmith & City C Stock are the first trains to be converted to one-person-operation by abolishing the guard and handing over door operation to the driver – part of a relentless reduction in staff numbers on all sections of the Underground to satisfy government imposed financial stringencies.

Docklands Light Railway

1987 The two branches from Tower Gateway and Stratford, both terminating at Island Gardens, opened on 31 August 1987.

Opening dates of stations, name changes and closures

Stations opened or first served by Underground trains

4.06.1984	Harrow & Wealdstone [BR]	BAKERLOO LINE *re-served*
4.06.1984	Kenton [BR]	BAKERLOO LINE *re-served*
4.06.1984	North Wembley [BR]	BAKERLOO LINE *re-served*
4.06.1984	South Kenton [BR]	BAKERLOO LINE *re-served*
4.06.1984	Wembley Central [BR]	BAKERLOO LINE *re-served*
7.04.1986	Kensington (Olympia)	DISTRICT LINE *regular service*
12.04.1986	Heathrow Terminal 4	PICCADILLY LINE

Stations opened on the Docklands Light Railway

31.08.1987	All Saints
31.08.1987	Bow Church
31.08.1987	Crossharbour
31.08.1987	Devons Road
31.08.1987	Heron Quays
31.08.1987	Island Gardens
31.08.1987	Limehouse
31.08.1987	Mudchute *first site*
31.08.1987	Poplar
31.08.1987	South Quay
31.08.1987	Tower Gateway
31.08.1987	Westferry
31.08.1987	West India Quay

Station names changed

	from	*to*
3.09.1983	Heathrow Central	Heathrow Central Terminals 1,2,3
12.04.1986	Heathrow Central Terminals 1,2,3	Heathrow Terminals 1,2,3
24.10.1989	Surrey Docks	Surrey Quays

Stations last served by Underground trains

31.10.1981	Blake Hall	CENTRAL LINE
24.09.1982	Bushey [BR]	BAKERLOO *retains BR service*
24.09.1982	Carpenders Park [BR]	BAKERLOO *retains BR service*
24.09.1982	Harrow & Wealdstone [BR]	BAKERLOO *retains BR service*
24.09.1982	Hatch End [BR]	BAKERLOO *retains BR service*
24.09.1982	Headstone Lane [BR]	BAKERLOO *retains BR service*
24.09.1982	Kenton [BR]	BAKERLOO *retains BR service*
24.09.1982	South Kenton [BR]	BAKERLOO *retains BR service*
24.09.1982	North Wembley [BR]	BAKERLOO *retains BR service*
24.09.1982	Watford High Street [BR]	BAKERLOO *retains BR service*
24.09.1982	Watford Junction [BR]	BAKERLOO *retains BR service*
24.09.1982	Wembley Central [BR]	BAKERLOO *retains BR service*

1 January   31 December
1981–1990

System on
31 December 1990

UNDERGROUND

Key to Lines		
Bakerloo	Metropolitan	
Central	Northern	
Circle	Piccadilly	
District	Victoria	
East London	Docklands Light Railway	
Hammersmith & City	≷ British Rail	
Jubilee	Waterloo & City	

Key to symbols

O Interchange stations
≷ Connections with British Rail
✈ Airport interchange

TPD I.MMIII

Principal developments of the decade

Central Line

1994 North Weald and Ongar stations closed when the passenger train service was withdrawn from the single-line Epping to Ongar branch on 30 September.

Docklands Light Railway

1991 The branch from Shadwell to Bank opened on 29 January.

1994 The section between Poplar and Beckton opened on 28 March.

1995 The link between Poplar and Westferry was brought into use.

1999 The section under the River Thames to Greenwich and Lewisham opened on 20 November.

Jubilee Line

1999 The extension from south of Bond Street to Stratford opened on 20 November. From that date the link with Charing Cross closed.

Piccadilly Line

1994 Aldwych station and the branch from Holborn was closed on 30 September.

Waterloo & City Line

1994 Ownership and operation was transferred from British Rail to London Underground on 1 April.

Opening dates of stations, name changes and closures

Stations opened or first served by Underground trains

14.05.1999	Canning Town	JUBILEE LINE
14.05.1999	North Greenwich	JUBILEE LINE
14.05.1999	Stratford	JUBILEE LINE
14.05.1999	West Ham	JUBILEE LINE
19.08.1999	Canada Water	EAST LONDON LINE
17.09.1999	Bermondsey	JUBILEE LINE
17.09.1999	Canada Water	JUBILEE LINE
17.09.1999	Canary Wharf	JUBILEE LINE
24.09.1999	Waterloo	JUBILEE LINE
7.10.1999	London Bridge	JUBILEE LINE
20.11.1999	Southwark	JUBILEE LINE
22.12.1999	Westminster	JUBILEE LINE

Stations opened or first served by DLR trains

29.01.1991	Bank
28.03.1994	Beckton
28.03.1994	Beckton Park
28.03.1994	Blackwall
28.03.1994	Custom House
28.03.1994	Cyprus
28.03.1994	East India
28.03.1994	Prince Regent
28.03.1994	Royal Albert
28.03.1994	Royal Victoria
28.11.1994	Gallions Reach
02.1996	Pudding Mill Lane
20.11.1999	Elverson Road
20.11.1999	Greenwich
20.11.1999	Lewisham
20.11.1999	Mudchute *re-sited*

Station names changed

	from	*to*
1994	Crossharbour	Crossharbour & London Arena

Stations last served by Underground or DLR trains

30.09.1994	Aldwych	PICCADILLY LINE
30.09.1994	North Weald	CENTRAL LINE
30.09.1994	Ongar	CENTRAL LINE
14.11.1999	Charing Cross	JUBILEE LINE
19.11.1999	Mudchute	DLR *original site*

Two of the impressive stations built for the Jubilee Line extension to Stratford are Canary Wharf *above* and North Greenwich *right*.

Far right The last train on the Central Line Ongar branch stops for photographs at North Weald.

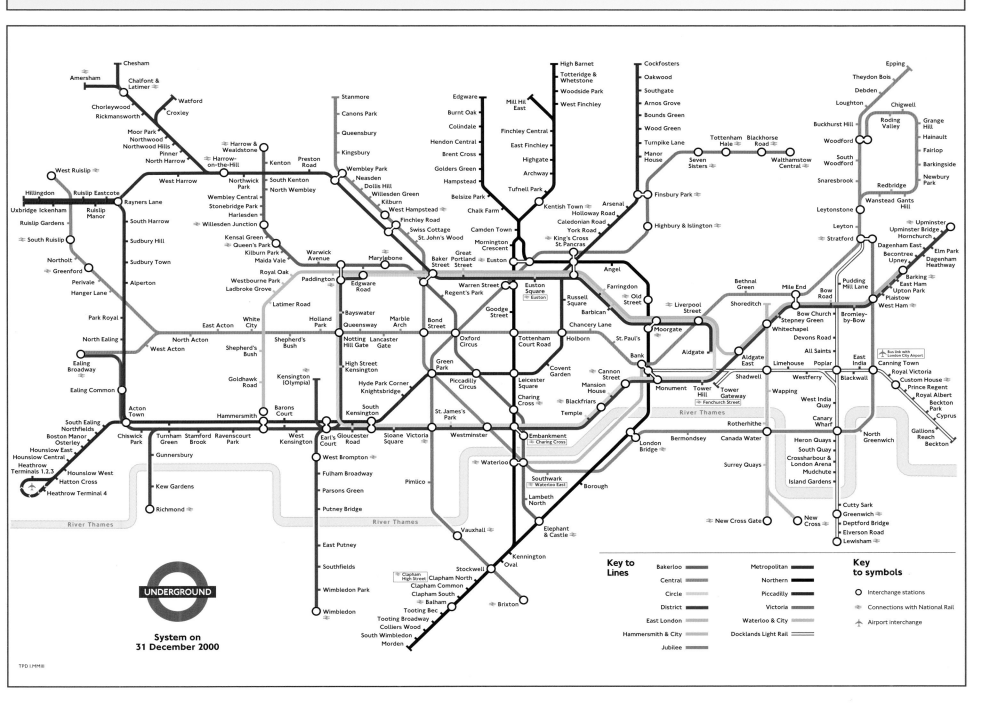

1 January   31 December

1991–2000

UNDERGROUND

**System on
31 December 2000**

Key to Lines			
Bakerloo		Metropolitan	
Central		Northern	
Circle		Piccadilly	
District		Victoria	
East London		Waterloo & City	
Hammersmith & City		Docklands Light Rail	
Jubilee			

Key to symbols

○ Interchange stations

≷ Connections with National Rail

✈ Airport interchange

A possible future London Underground

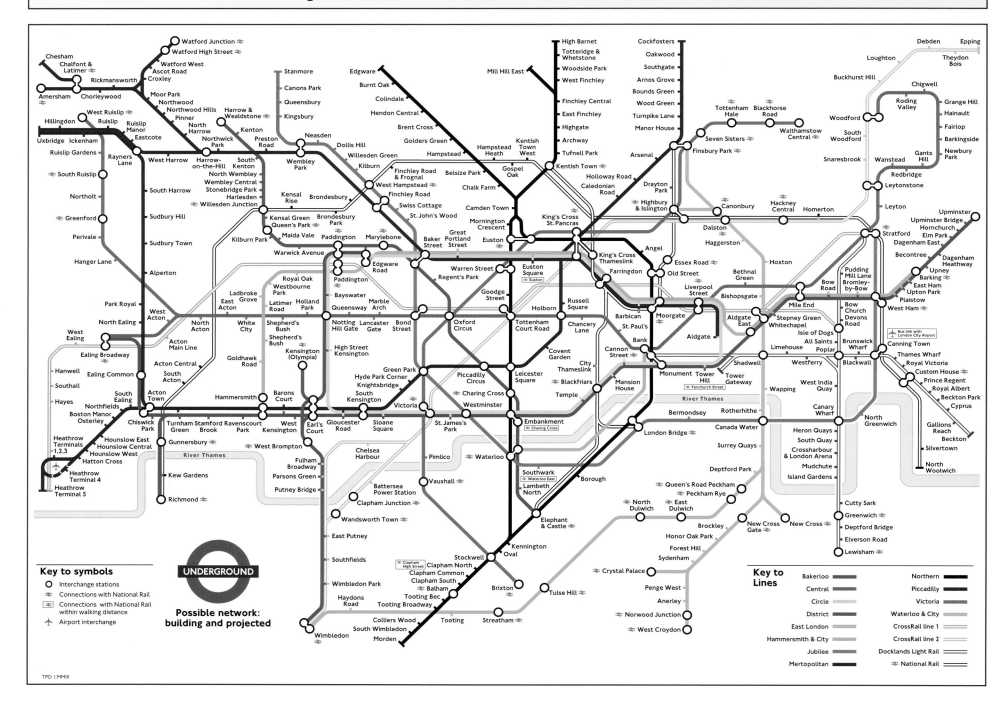

Key to symbols

○ Interchange stations
⇌ Connections with National Rail
🔲 Connections with National Rail within walking distance
✈ Airport interchange

UNDERGROUND

Possible network: building and projected

Key to Lines

Bakerloo		Northern	
Central		Piccadilly	
Circle		Victoria	
District		Waterloo & City	
East London		CrossRail line 1	
Hammersmith & City		CrossRail line 2	
Jubilee		Docklands Light Rail	
Mertopolitan		National Rail	

TPD I.MMIII